MIGRATIONS

For my mother, Marcelina Padilla; stepfather, Eliseo Rivera;
in-laws, Arcelia López and Efrain Vera, and the countless
other pioneros, whose migrations have had a significant impact
on our history, culture, and lives.

MIGRATIONS

J.L. Torres

This is a LARB Libros publication
Published by The Los Angeles Review of Books
6671 Sunset Blvd., Suite 1521, Los Angeles, CA 90028
www.larbbooks.org

These stories from the collection were originally published in the following publications, sometimes in earlier versions: "The Adventures of Macho the Dwarf, Or an Allegory of Epic Proportions about a Little Person," in the *T.J. Eckleburg Review* (web); "Clemente Burning," the *Killens Review of Arts & Letters*; "Go Make Some Fire" (as "Lost Tribe"), *Acentos* (web); "Rip and Reck into that Good Light," *Harper's Ferry Review*.

ISBN 978-1-940660-74-5

Library of Congress Control Number: 2021936023

Migration is the story of my body.

—Victor Hernández Cruz, *Red Beans*

CONTENTS

MINT CONDITION

THEY LOST THEIR SIGNAL on the highway and never regained it. A few months after the hurricane, the coverage was spotty at best. Of all the hassles they experienced during the recovery, the phone situation was what bothered Brett the most. Nikki had bigger problems than phone service, especially losing Jim a few months before Maria hit. She wasn't a phone person anyway, so as usual she left her phone at home. She told Brett to charge his before they left, but he forgot to do it.

She had never visited Dorado or attended the annual event there that her husband never missed, but it wasn't hard to get lost on the island. At the first sign to the town, she exited onto a rotary, curved past a fountain with three giant sea horses and entered a two-lane road that curled up into the distance and disappeared into a cluster of trees. The other way, it spiraled down toward some knobby hills. They parked on the side of the road, next to an electrical power station, to get their bearings and check their signal.

No coverage, and the battery was dead. What sounded like a two-stroke chainsaw buzzed from somewhere close. There were no road signs to Dorado anywhere. The road looked like it would be busy normally, but chunks of it were gone. Splintered utility poles and blue-tarped roofs on beaten houses covered the landscape. She also spotted what looked like a dive, your standard chinchorro that served fritters and beer. They got back into the car and drove toward the hills. They were both hungry, and she could use a cold one. Besides, they could ask for directions to the resort.

When they parked, the people sitting outside gawked. It wasn't every day you saw a 1952 Cadillac Eldorado. It's like going back in time, an elderly woman shouted. Without water and electricity, we *are* living in the past, a man at the bar commented. That made everyone laugh. Entering the place, Nikki realized the chain saw noise was a generator going full blast. The restaurant was near a power station but had no grid electricity. The entire neighborhood had no electricity. The owner was doing his best to satisfy the line of customers. They sat outside. It was windy and overcast.

As they were looking over the menu, a woman ran clumsily toward them in flip-flops. Everyone in the restaurant watched as she ran with her hands on her head, crying loudly and asking for help. The owner went up to her, and from the way he talked to her it was obvious he knew who she was. Between sobs, she babbled something about her neighbor.

Nikki got up and went to the woman, saw she was disheveled and in shock, and ran back to the car to grab her nurse's medical kit from the trunk. *Take me to him* she said and turned around to tell Brett to stay put. Nikki followed the woman, accompanied by the owner of the restaurant and a crowd of rubberneckers. The woman led them past her house to the neighbor's. The shack's corrugated tin roof had blown away, replaced by a FEMA-administered blue tarp with a corner flapping in the wind. She told them she had been bringing him some lunch and guided them through a house full of candles and buckets of water, toward the man's backyard.

A few gasps greeted the old man's slender body hanging from a ceiba tree, quiet and at rest. His opened mouth drooped; his eyes straining to leave his skull fixed a sadness to his face. A few feet away lay a small wooden ladder. Two men brought him down and set him on the ground. Before they did, Nikki noticed the pants soiled with urine and the man's erection, and she knew he was dead. She checked his ABC's anyway and then whispered to the owner that he was dead and to call 911. Without a signal, the owner had to order an employee to drive to the police station.

Nikki noticed the woman crying and reassured her that he probably was dead when she found him. The young woman, eyes red from crying, responded, I'm only eighteen, I shouldn't have to see that. Nikki nodded and patted her shoulder, thinking she looked much older. She was grateful Brett hadn't seen it.

Back at the restaurant, they ordered food, although Nikki was not hungry. Brett asked what happened, but she didn't want to talk about it. He had a hearty appetite. She drank her warm beer and picked pieces of roast pork from Brett's plate. She thought about the many deaths she had witnessed or heard about at the hospital in the past few months. People who couldn't get proper medical care under the post-storm conditions. Suicides were on the rise.

While paying the bill, Nikki asked for directions to the resort. The owner thanked her for helping out, even though it was too late. Tino was old and alone, he explained. His wife died two months after the hurricane and like many others in town, he didn't have electricity. She just nodded; it was her duty.

He spouted directions, delivered with hand gestures and important landmarks to remember along the way. She had to drive in the opposite direction, toward the trees. As they were walking back to the car, there was a sudden whirring sound and the dangling lights on the restaurant's awning came on. The power had returned and everyone in the restaurant cheered and applauded. Praise God, a woman yelled. The generator went off and the jukebox ignited with "Despacito." A few couples started dancing, holding drinks and each other equally tight.

Even with the directions in her head, Nikki had to stop a few times and ask strangers. Along the way they saw a pickup truck stacked with blue vats of water. It was coming from the center of the island, where people had set up makeshift water stations made of pipes running between forks of trees and upheld by poles. Dozens of people stopped by and loaded up on the rainwater flowing down from the mountains. She had gone with a medical team to assist the people up there, whom a doctor called the forgotten ones. Jim didn't live to see the hurricane, and maybe it was for the best. He wasn't the ideal person to have around in a crisis. Ever since college, Jim Willson's focus was on carpeing the diem. On his charge toward making fast money and living out his hedonistic pleasures, planning wasn't the priority. In business, he was smart and lucky. Right out of college, he took a job at Goldman Sachs and worked long enough to cash out company stock a few years before the 2008 crisis. With that considerable loot, and a robust pension, he moved Nikki and Brett to Puerto Rico.

The island had always held an allure of exotica and paradise for him. His first trip there had been with Nikki, after their relationship became serious and she wanted him to meet her family. He fell in love with the tropical weather, the sunsets at the beach, the people and food. It was the leisurely life for him, a Midwesterner who hadn't seen a beach until he arrived in New York city to begin his career. He bought some beach properties, hired someone to manage the rentals, and spent time hopping from one to another for weeks on end. After years in Puerto Rico, he claimed the moniker "beach bum in paradise" with pride. The El D's vanity plates read BCHBUM.

Nikki never questioned her husband's desire to enjoy life to the fullest. That actually attracted her to him. She came from a family of austere individuals who liked Jim but didn't completely approve of his libertine ways. They met at a club in New York, where they danced and talked until daybreak. Back then, she only wanted to have fun, and he reeked of fun. He kept calling her and she kept answering the phone, thinking that it was all about fun, assuming it would not lead to anything because he was ten years older. She can't pinpoint the moment it turned. Time together blurred everything, and soon she found herself caring for him. She obsessed about him, perhaps way too much, and got excited just hearing the phone ring. Hearing his voice again brought her happiness and solace.

She dreaded moving to Puerto Rico. She tried to talk him out of it. They had great jobs in New York. He had an enviable job at Goldman Sachs, and she worked at Mount Sinai. They had a beautiful home in Westchester County. And the truth was she did not like the island. Her parents had moved back after they retired, but she told them flat out it wasn't for her. Deep down, she understood the depth of her assimilation was irreversible.

The few times she had visited Puerto Rico had been awful. Guys she met there were testosterone-driven, immature jerks. Everybody was so judgmental, especially about Nuyoricans like her, who knew nothing about the country's history and spoke Spanglish. Not being a fan of the sun, even the beaches didn't impress her. Because she visited family in small towns, the boredom was unbearable for a city girl like her. When Jim told her his plans to move, she balked. But he was always persuasive. Perhaps she deferred to his maturity and experience, thinking he knew better. He closed the deal when he showed her photos of the condo he had bought in San Juan. If she was going to live in Puerto Rico, at least it would be in the capital city.

Looking back, she regretted not intervening in his disregard for his health. He drank and smoked too much, and he didn't exactly have a healthy diet. His idea of exercise was pushing a hammock to rock himself to sleep. She kept nagging about getting checkups, eating healthier, but he didn't listen. He wouldn't even let her take his blood pressure.

It caught up to him, and she was barely a widow when she had to deal with the worst hurricane to ever hit the island. A day before the storm, she and Brett flew to New York to stay with family. Nikki knew their condo was not adequately prepared, and she didn't have the time or know-how to do anything about it. Jim believed people overreacted to hurricanes and never bought the aluminum storm panels that everyone bought. Hurricanes never hit San Juan that much, anyway, he used to say. Then he would always talk about how tornadoes were worse.

Maria blew out two windows in the condo. The furniture was wet and tossed around like garbage. Nikki salvaged whatever piece of furniture she could and had the rest removed. She bought new furniture, had the windows fixed, and ordered aluminum shutters. It took weeks and many phone calls to buy and have a generator and water tank shipped from the US—items she had often asked Jim to buy but he dismissed as unnecessary, although they experienced routine water and electrical shortages. Days after the hurricane, lines at gas stations and supermarkets were long and everybody's nerves were shot. The ATMs didn't work so she also had to wait on slow-moving lines at the bank just to get cash. As weeks went by without electricity and water, every day became a struggle just to eat, to have potable water, and maintain sanity.

Living in San Juan made it easier. They got power and water sooner than others. But Nikki had to handle her husband's unattended affairs, including the '52 Eldorado. A car that cost too much in upkeep and was too valuable to drive every day. Jim once commented that both she and the car had a lot in common: both were classically beautiful, had amazing contours, and required high maintenance.

Brett wanted the car. She had a difficult time explaining to him that was not an option. At sixteen, he just didn't have the resources to take care of it properly, and she wasn't going to do it for him until he could. Besides, he simply wasn't responsible enough. He didn't like hearing any of that and pouted for weeks. It meant a lot to him, she understood. That old car was one of the few things that connected Brett to a dad who had been there, but really hadn't been.

At first, she just wanted to get rid of it. It was taking up their extra space in the condo's parking lot. And to be honest, with all that was happening, the car pissed her off every time she looked at it. She even thought of giving it away, but her father told her she was crazy to do that. Apparently, the car would bring in good money. In mint condition, the car was worth over two hundred fifty thousand. She had to see the figures for herself to believe it. With that kind of money, she could move back to the states, save some for Brett's college.

Then, cleaning up Jim's desk, she found the tickets to the annual Eldorado Club de Puerto Rico Show and Gala. Every year Jim took the cover off the car and drove it to Dorado to meet up with other El D enthusiasts. They always included an extra ticket for a spouse or significant other, but she didn't want to spend a rare free day hanging around old cars and older men talking about them. It seemed strange that under the post-storm situation, they would hold the event, but she called to confirm, and they informed her it was still on.

She asked Brett if he wanted to see a bunch of old cars like his dad's. He didn't seem thrilled. The past few weeks he would shut himself in his room more often than usual, lying on the floor and staring at the ceiling while listening to The Movielife's "Mercy Is Asleep at the Wheel" or LCD Soundsystem's "American Dream." Mostly, he spent hours playing video games. She usually put a limit on the game playing, but he had been going through a rough patch. He needed to get out of the house, take a shower occasionally, and get some sun and exercise, and there was no way she was going to let him stay home alone for two days. He perked up a bit when she told him there were pools, water parks, and other things to explore at the resort. So, they packed for the two-day event, dusted off the El D and took to the road. Years ago, Jim had brought home the gold cup for first prize. She figured one of those guys might want to buy an award-winning car.

They reached the front gate of the resort, after a few pit stops for directions and restrooms, and to gas up again because the old car was a guzzler. They had driven through deforested areas more like a dystopian winterland than the tropics. More blue tarps on roughed-up houses; then suddenly, dense gated communities full of luxury homes. Everywhere, there was the stink of rotten vegetation and piles of debris skirting roads brown from sewage.

At the resort's entrance, Nikki showed the security guard the tickets and asked where to go for the event. He brushed his hand toward the direction and opened the gate.

The event was on what once was a century-old fruit plantation. The resort retained parts of the hacienda's architecture, the most striking of which was an enormous water wheel. Eleven Eldorados were parked under its shadow, twelve with Nikki's 1952 black convertible. By far, hers was the oldest. The next closest was a red 1968 model. She drove behind an attendant with a tablet who guided her into her designated parking spot. Once parked, she asked, Where are the other cars? With a sigh of relief, the attendant said she was the last one. Your room will be ready after the buffet, he told them. Then, he tossed their bags in a golf cart and drove off.

From the car, they saw people gathered a few yards from the other El D's. Men and women, dressed casually but stylish, drank champagne, nibbled hors d'oeuvres, and chatted under an elegant tent. Brett scanned the area, in awe. The wheel itself was monumental, but the huge arches alongside it, remnants of the hacienda's aqueduct, were equally impressive. Water spouted into a pool, one of many interconnected waterways. Farther down, up some stairs, a small pavilion stood where the buffet would take place. Everything looked pristine and whispered of money and opulence. Everywhere, gorgeous royal palm trees graced the grounds. Not one touched by Maria's wrath.

Nikki didn't know anyone. A squat man with a goatee came over to the car. They both got out of the car to meet him. He wore a guayabera and a stick-on name tag. He introduced himself as Miguel Ontiveros, the President of the Club. She shook his soft, manicured hand, and apologetically he mentioned that he recognized the '52 El D but not her. No one would know her, she understood that. But apparently, no one in the club knew about Jim's passing. Not Ontiveros, when she told him, nor anyone else wearing a name tag whom he called over to talk to her. Jim didn't keep in touch much with other members. A shame, they all repeated, because they all liked him. More than one person called him the life of the party or a live wire.

Jim could be charming, this she knew. He told a good story, could put anyone in a party mood, and occasionally told a raunchy joke, to her dismay. They kept calling him the life of the party, which annoyed her. The way they smiled afterward, looking at each other, privy to some inside joke, made her uneasy.

Ontiveros called everyone to the pavilion for the buffet. Inside, a string quartet played Pachelbel's Canon as everyone filed past the various food stations, and servers dressed in crisp, white linen uniforms spooned their plates with all types of delicacies. Nikki and Brett sat alone at a table. There were chairs and tables, but mostly everyone stood with plates in hand, talking and eating, wine glasses resting at arm's length. It soon became clear to Nikki that she had entered a clique space. These folks knew each other, did business with each other. Had been doing it for years, perhaps entire careers. Probably the only reason why they came together around a bunch of classic cars. An excuse to network and close a deal they had been working on for months, maybe years. The air smelled of quid pro quo. She didn't belong here. Her husband once did, but she was the Invisible Wife. The widow who came too late to the party. She had to circulate if she was going to sell the car.

She excused herself, scolded Brett not to eat with his eyes, and went over to Ontiveros. El Presidente was in a good mood after sev- eral whiskeys. He was laughing it up with a tall bleached redhead, touching her arm more than his wife would have liked, if she had been there. Nikki politely entered the conversation and told him about selling the '52 El D.

You know anyone interested?

How much are you asking? Gloria, the redhead, asked.

Two hundred k, Nikki said, quoting the book value. They both laughed and shook their heads.

No way you'd get that, Gloria said, in a tone laced with pity.

Nikki looked at them, confused. It won an award from this club, didn't it?

That was long ago, Ontiveros responded. And the car isn't even in mint condition.

Or to be more exact, Gloria corrected, in Concours d'Elegance status, the highest level of value.

This was all shocking to Nikki, who assumed the car was in great shape. She returned to her table upset. As the evening progressed, word got around, and a few men approached her about the car.

There was Luis Aguirre, a banker, who made his sales pitch too close to her for comfort. At one point, she had to tell him, "My breasts are not part of the transaction." He laughed at that.

Okay, let me break it down for you, he said. Yes, it's not only a classic El D. It's one of a handful. The concept car for the El D's that would follow. But Jim didn't take care of it. He paused and looked at her with a lech smile. Maybe Jim hadn't taken care of all his business. Nikki's desire to retch was only surpassed by her suppressed desire to slap him or laugh, or both.

Tell you what. I'll buy it for a fraction of the fair value to help you out.

Aguirre told her to seriously think about his offer and tossed his business card on the table. Brett snorted and called him a jerk after he pointed at them with two forefingers and swaggered away. Nikki shook her head. He was offering less than the cost of his gaudy Rolex. She tore his card to pieces.

The real estate developer, Guillermo—call me Guillo—Martinez, offered even less because he would have to invest thousands to bring the car to Concours value. He told her he had always loved Jim's car.

I asked him to sell it to me several times because the neglect on the car… He lowered his head and looked away. Nikki wondered, *Is he going to cry?* It was just sad, he said, to anyone who loves Eldorados. It's car abuse.

Nikki couldn't believe it. You know, she told Martinez, I'm getting the feeling all you guys are trying to take advantage of me because I'm a woman.

Mrs. Willson, if you want, I'll show you.

She stared at him. Okay, sure, go ahead.

They walked back to where the cars stood under filtered light like museum pieces. He popped the hood and pointed to the accumulating rust, the chipped parts, and frayed hoses. Like a fussy mother-in-law, he ran a finger along the motor. Look at the grease and dirt, he said, shaking his head. He showed her minute scratches all over the car. A muffler that needed replacement. That upholstery, he pointed. It's fading, see? When he finished, she was happy he was not gloating.

He handed her a business card and headed to the bar. She was embarrassed, and furious with herself, for not having someone inspect the car first. Angry with Jim for not taking care of the one possession he bragged about more than anything else. The redhead, Gloria, came over and plopped herself at their table. Brett was on his second dessert. She had a pouty face and even reached out to cradle and squeeze Nikki's hand.

Guillo just told me about the condition of the car, Gloria said. It's not news to anybody in the club. She looked around, suddenly getting serious. We warned Jim the car was deteriorating and needed work, but he didn't listen. He just wanted to drive it. *Trophies don't mean a damn thing to me*, he said. She lowered her voice to mimic Nikki's dead husband.

With a tilt of her head and a smile, Gloria entered some nostalgic place. Jim used to get drunk and drive the car in circles, to everyone's horror, she said. Not so much that he could get hurt, but because he could damage that classic American icon and our cars. A few times, early in the morning we found him in the car sleeping off a hangover. He loved cars like everyone else in the club. He would tell us stories about his first car, a beat-up Mustang that he eventually drove into a ditch. How he loved driving it down the highway with no destination in mind. How his favorite uncle left him the El D in his will, hoping the responsibility of taking care of a Cadillac would help Jim mature.

The last few years, he came to this event just to party, definitely not to compete or network. He had enough money, he would tell everyone, and he wasn't going to waste the rest of his life plodding and scheming for more. Gloria trilled with laughter at that and then looked at Nikki again, her eyes softening. I'll buy the car, she offered. After seeing Nikki's surprised face, she told her, I'm a woman of means.

Her claim to wealth didn't surprise Nikki. The diamond watch on her elegant wrist and Akoya pearl necklace dangling around her bust line gave it credibility. She didn't understand why Gloria would want to buy a classic car that was losing monetary value. That thought bothered her, along with the stories she told about Jim. Stories that he never shared with her. She didn't know how he got the Eldorado. Didn't know that he was his Uncle Bob's favorite nephew. He hardly spoke two sentences about his uncle. What Mustang?

Nikki thanked her for the offer and said she would consider it, along with the others. It was the highest offer, but nothing close to what she thought she was going to get. Gloria gave her a card, too. Nikki recognized the family name, people who owned various businesses, old money in Puerto Rico. The patriarch, long dead, founded the first cement manufacturing company on the island. Nikki was now certain she did not like Gloria much, nor did she care for her offer, which could have been considerably higher.

She downed the last sip of Bordeaux and told Brett they were going to their hotel room. He seemed eager to go. As they were exiting, a young man with a bushy beard, sporting a pork pie hat, and dressed in tight wrinkled clothing, ran up to her. Animated and excited, he explained how much he loved the '52 El D and offered her twenty bitcoins for it. Nikki didn't understand he was offering her the best deal. She didn't know anything about bitcoins and thought it was a mean joke, one she was not in the mood to hear.

She shoved him out of the way. He picked up his hat from the ground, and yelled, you're making a big mistake. Bitcoins are the future. She flipped him the finger, and Brett laughed.

Their room was spacious and full of the amenities expected from an exclusive and expensive resort. It was more like a small, lavish, and well-stocked apartment. She wondered why she never came along on these excursions with Jim. Nursing was a profession where double shifts were common. Sometimes you had no choice, but she could have made the time. If anything, it was a waste of their club membership, which now reviewing the bills that Jim paid, at times late, she realized was quite a small fortune. As large as the room was, she felt claustrophobic in it. She opened the curtains to a view of lush greenery topped by a gray sky streaked with eerie purple hues.

Brett had turned on the widescreen TV and was fiddling with the remote. She grabbed it out of his hands.

Get your lazy ass out of bed, she screamed. Go take a walk or go swim.

He just hung his head and flopped backward on the bed. She closed her fists in front of her, closed her eyes. Okay, shouldn't have screamed at you. She took a quick, deep breath and exhaled.

She stormed out of the room. Downstairs, she inquired the concierge about the botanical spa. He picked up the phone and made the arrangements, including a driver to take her there.

She walked past a gigantic tree, enormous branches extended out in all directions like crooked, wanting fingers. Graceful lights dangled from them like puppets on strings. They brightened the stairs to the entrance of an A-frame building with a terracotta roof. Past the large, heavy Spanish doors, Nikki entered a foyer fragrant with herbs and flowers hanging from breaking-neck high rafters or sitting on mahogany shelves and marble top counters. The space glowed with soft lights, and serenity and tranquility immediately claimed her body.

A young woman, her "therapist," welcomed her. She led her to a dressing room with lockers and handed her a white robe. Nikki slowly undressed and peeked at the wall mirror. Not bad, she thought. Even with a few pounds, she looked healthy. She noticed the tiny varicose veins, some cellulite dimples. Perhaps, the belly was getting a bit soft. She tried to work out, but sometimes the schedule intervened. Tried to eat a good diet, but life, so hectic, so impatient, just didn't cooperate.

Jim once called her body a wonderland. Way before John Mayer stole it from him, he would joke. The wonder for her husband faded with the years. Sometimes Nikki thought maybe it was because she demanded he get a vasectomy after having such a difficult childbirth with Brett. He resisted and only relented after she threaten to leave him. But it probably started before that, when she wanted to go back to work. He always had this vision of them hanging out at the beach forever. They had the money, for sure, but the beach life didn't fulfill her. Or maybe, Jim was just getting listless after years pursuing paradise.

The therapist returned and guided her past a reflection pool to one of the outdoor pavilions. It was an airy place, with billowing white gossamer fabric running across the ceiling. All the furniture had a rustic, hacienda look. She undressed and lay on the table, and the therapist covered her with a large towel. She lit some herbs on a bowl atop of a strange figurine that looked like a Taino god. It had a large smile, bulging round eyes, and large ears. Naked, it had a nub of a penis.

The therapist worked the oil and herbs deep into her muscles. Nikki couldn't keep her eyes off the idol's creepy smile and hypnotic eyes. She closed her own eyes tight and concentrated on the birds' chirps and whistles. The idol figure started laughing, a piercing cackle, its unblinking eyes heavy and oppressive. They pinned her body down to the table. She wanted to scream but nothing came out of her mouth. The therapist's light touch on her shoulder broke the daymare. She handed her the robe and asked if she needed help to the pool.

Although groggy, Nikki responded, I'm fine, and the young woman left. Sitting on the table, she closed her eyes and inhaled the aroma of plants and wildflowers mixed with the incense floating through the room. Robed, she walked toward the pool, making sure not to glance back at the idol. The pool area was restricted to women. It was empty, so she disrobed and waded in.

The bubbling hot water tickled her skin. She breathed slowly, sensing her heart beat steadily. After a few moments in the hot water, she plunged into the icy pool, letting out a sharp squeal as she did. Every part of her body pulsed and tingled. She sat for a few minutes in the cold water. If she could only stay in this place for a few months, she thought. Or maybe forever.

Back at the hotel room, they opted for room service. Brett had taken her advice, or maybe he was just bored, and went out for a swim at the pool. He forgot to put sunscreen and was burnt, but he enjoyed himself. Visibly drained, he soon turned over and fell asleep.

He dreamed he drove the El D to the beach, doused it with gasoline and set it on fire. It exploded into flames. Inside, his father smiled and waved. A band of drummers and masqueraded revelers, led by a dwarf, locked arms and danced around the car. Brett joined them. In the moonlight, they passed bottles of wine and danced, until the car was ashes and the drummers' hands bled.

The spa had made Nikki so relaxed she thought she would fall out too. But she couldn't stop thinking about the car. They were supposed to parade the cars around the resort. Nikki knew that wasn't going to happen. Neither would the evening gala when they gave out all the prizes. She flipped channels and found a romantic comedy, but minutes into it her mind drifted. Images of Jim in the El D flooded her mind. She didn't know where these images were coming from. Home videos? Photos? Memories? In all of them, he was never smiling. He was always alone. Then, right before she gave in to sleep, she saw herself and Brett in the car, floating on the ocean back to New York.

The next morning, they packed their stuff and ate a big breakfast. They jumped into a golf cart and the valet drove them to the water wheel. The area glittered with colorful balloons and streamers, and under a tent the wait staff stood with their backs to the food and drink. The cars, except hers, were lined for the parade. But the owners, El Presidente and Gloria included, were staring at the sky. A band was hired to play salsa and merengue, but the musicians held their instruments in silence. They, along with the crowd, gaped at the numerous black birds on the top of the huge arches.

Those are the biggest grackles, I've ever seen, commented a bald-headed man with glasses. Nikki didn't know about grackles, but she had seen enough crows to know when she saw one. Soon, the distinct cawing began. She, like the others, did not know the Puerto Rican crow had been extinct for centuries. Brett marveled at the big, black birds. He found them shiny and beautiful.

They cut through the crowd and back to the Eldorado. As they approached it, a crow flew right over their heads and plopped on the hood and stood there. They watched from a few feet away. For a moment, they and the crow stared at each other. Another crow flew overhead and landed beside it. The first crow squawked, then both flew away. They watched the crows disappear, looked at each other, and then got in the Eldorado. Only one way to go this time.

SUCIO

YOU WERE A SUCIO, and you knew it. Your father was one, your three brothers raised the standard. Your grandfather is in the Sucieria Hall of Fame. In fact, your entire male lineage going back to the Stone Age probably was a bunch of guys who couldn't keep their junk from getting them into trouble. When the stand-up cavemen were out hunting to feed the tribe, your male ancestor was banging somebody's old lady as soon as she bent to gather. When the Crusaders marched off to liberate the Holy Land, your guys stayed behind for the leftovers. You shudder to think what they may have been doing during the Plague. Famine, pestilence, war, death, it didn't matter. The male bloods in your tribe rode behind plowing through women and not caring who it hurt, like it was a birthright.

That's what the machos in your family believe. They taught you to be a sucio. Not to cry, especially over no woman. Screw 'em and leave 'em, right? You didn't question, and you learned. But sooner or later karma had to catch up to somebody, somehow. Guess that'd be you, the only one in recent memory who had any conscience about using your penis as the frontal lobe of your brain. You had the audacity to be sweet to bitches who'd dump you. That was the first sign. Sitting around listening to boleros when you were crushing for some mami. Another sign.

Then you met her, the love interest, la femme fatale, the anima: Sari. She, who attended to your bruises and cracked bones from your latest beatdown, this one bigger than any other whoopin' in the history of sucios getting smacked down. Another reason for your funk. The amount of violence directed at you for taking care of a slacker's business appalled you. Those mofos should be thanking you for taking care of their business. You always said if it's not being tilled, someone has to do it, or it goes to weeds. In the Sucio Code that was like a commandment, but you knew the risks of sucieria, understood the consequences if you were confronted either by the other guy or your vieja or worse, a *Fatal Attraction* copycat. Shit will hit the fan, sooner or later, and like your dishonorable ancestors, you never had a plan.

It's like genetically you were programmed to be perverso but estupido. Whatever you got extra in penis size the good Lord subtracted from the dinosaur brain you inherited. Your brother Mangú called you soft all the time. Take martial arts classes, Amador, a man's got to learn to protect himself, he'd say. But you didn't listen because you thought he had nothing to teach you. Thought his mind was getting frizzed from the feminine scents he kept sniffing off his fingers.

True, this beatdown was epic, really tragic. You had bad ones before. Like that time you got caught fondling that drag queen you thought was just another girl on your jock. Bad enough your gender radar was way off, but then her bf and crew, who looked like they walked off the set of *Drag Race*, made sure to have your ass handed to you. Or when that Rican knocked you out cold and tossed your sorry ass into a dumpster for hitting on his girlfriend. You could have walked away but you started saying nasty lies about how slutty she was. You can't remember how many times you been smacked in the face, how many drinks tossed in your face, sometimes both at the same time.

And you're getting sloppier, if that's possible. Dude found you in bed with his wife. How clichéd is that? You couldn't plan it better? Or listened to the bitch when she told you to make it fast cause the old man's gonna come home soon? Didn't you know cuernú worked out and kept in considerably better shape than you will ever be in? Six feet, three inches and jacked, hands the size of two perniles, and at that moment fueled by righteous anger over his wife sleeping with someone like you. You owe your life to Ms. Cuernú and her loud screaming that snapped husband from his steroid induced, Hulk-like fury. Leaving you bloodied and broken on the mat of love like the loser in a '90s UFC match.

All that didn't matter, because when Sari walked into your hospital room, you thought the pain was worth it. Even with the drug-induced euphoria, you noticed that beautiful behind. Her cheeks round and sweet like ripe, plump honey dew melons on a hot Fourth of July picnic. You don't want to say something cheesy like Uranus, but it was of planetary proportions—maybe a dwarf one like Pluto—and even your addled brain could send enough stimuli to your guevo to make you hard. When she bent over to take your temperature you gazed at her mocha bosoms shaped like overripe papayas and suddenly got a craving for your mom's dulce de lechosa.

She was so generously stuffed into her nurse uniform that your delirious but perv mind imagined your crew had hired an escort to dress as a nurse and do you a solid. But Nurse Sari was all business, and as you healed and regained consciousness you put on a full court press that she evaded like LeBron slipping through the Knicks' defense. Homegirl did not mess. She found out the how and why behind your Super Smackdown. You one sorry suciopath, she said, peeling off your fingers from her hand in disgust, like they were slimy slugs. Then she went on to inform you on what a miserable, pathetic, shallow piece of crap you are. Then like the genuine Heartbreaking Samurai she was, she dealt you the mortal blow.

Your wasted life is a disgrace to dying people everywhere, she said. Nothing new, but something about how she said it—with that look like she was going to puke. Maybe it was the drugs, or that you were spiraling down the macho chute way before you met Nurzilla. But tears flooded your eyes and you looked up at her and she laughed. Don't waste them puppy eyes on me, slick, she said. You weren't trying to get over on her, okay maybe a little, but for a moment you felt the twinge of regret that your life revolved around nothing more than satisfying the needs of your penis. For once, this realization shamed you, especially when you saw her tend to other patients, with genuine tenderness. When she talked so sweetly to the abuelita in the next bed, you wanted to cry. You didn't deserve someone like her, and that unhinged you.

The thought of a catastrophic fuku ruling your destiny began to haunt you. Why couldn't you be happy? Why did your penis have to dictate every aspect of your life? You wanted to turn it around. You were a modern man. Although your people came from hick towns in the mountains of DR and PR, you had transcended belief in fukus and voodoo. You grew up in the barrios of Long Island. You knew the real deal.

So, you set on a mission to win Sari over. Court her, dine her like a caballero, with honorable intentions. Old School. You wanted to crack the mental grip of all that cheating, lying, scurrying around in the night like a rat. Always playing the heavy in the drama. Damaging people for nothing more than a few minutes of meaningless sex. Yeah, Prime A sex. Mind exploding, supernatural, one hundred OMGs orgasmic sex, but there was always a trade-off, right? You wanted to settle down, become respectable, a family man who would teach his sons the lighted path toward decency and away from sucieria.

Sari had other plans. Shortly after your release from the hospital, you returned and handed her flowers, but she gave you no time to bare your soul. She threw them back at you, and they scattered all over the floor. Then she cursed you because she had to clean up the mess and told you to leave or she would call security.

This is a hospital, you idiot, she screamed. I got no time for your stupid nonsense.

You rode the 1 train back to the Heights, flower petals decorating your jacket. At home, you slumped into the ragged sofa and watched *When Harry Met Sally* while eating the five pounds of assorted Stover's chocolates you were going to give her. That's when it hit you, that you and your ancestors *were* cursed. What else could explain the painful, emotionally barren lives of you and your forebears. Every single one of them, even the halfway successful ones, waited for death hunched over bottle and shot glass.

This curse was some deep, serious stuff. You had no way out that you could see. You picked up your cell and made that booty call to your fav platanera, Annalisse. She wasn't into you, but girl regularly attended the Church of the Well Endowed. A sure thing, a slam dunk, but sista turned you down. First time, evah. That's when you knew things had hit Defcon 1.

Then, you met *him* at the Starbucks on W. 181st, the one near the Church. That's where you were sitting, sipping your café con leche, when he came out, newspaper under his arm, holding his venti decaf tall sugar-free vanilla caramel skinny ice macchiato. You had seen him in his usual corner, The Writer. That's what everybody in the hood called him. He was always pecking away on his laptop, deep in thought or into whatever book he was reading. Most times, he sat there scoping everything and everyone when he wasn't checking out the booty, his owlish eyes circling the place. Then, he'd scratch something in that banged-up purple spiral notebook. He looked possessed when he did that or tapped away on his laptop.

To be honest, dude didn't present much. Skinny, funky crusted hair tied in the shortest ponytail ever. Always in black, even on the hottest summer days. Those brown Gollum eyes, popping anytime he looked up, huddled over whatever he was doing. Nobody messed with The Writer. He didn't mess with anyone and seemed less harmless and bothersome than a fly. Dude looked smart and professional, so people respected him, though nobody in the hood trusted anyone who read that much. Like all that reading was gonna drive the mofo insane someday, a matter of time.

The Writer looked down at your sorry face and knew. He shook his head and was going to leave but you must have been the saddest case he ever saw of SDS—Sucio Depressed Syndrome. He sat down across from you.

Brah, you ain't lookin' too hot.

You didn't want to talk to nobody, especially no ferret-looking nerd.

I've known dudes like you all my life, been there myself, he said.

You smirked and turned toward the Chinese restaurant, thinking you'd be better off eating shrimp fried rice than listening to this fool trying to front.

You? Come on, bro.

What? You think a sucio has to present a certain way. I've probably landed more aviones in a week than you've seen in your entire life. It's not about looks, man, it's all about genetics. You and me both are engineered, wired to be hounds—I know. I write about it. It's no curse either, forget that BS. But you can bring it under control. You got to or it's gonna eat you alive. That woman's got you in a funk, yeah, that one, the special one you want to have your children—she will never, ever be yours less you do something drastic about your horny ways, brother. I'm speaking gospel truth.

He got up, tucked his newspaper under his armpit again.

You probably gonna keep playing your stupid game, getting beat down and dealing with all that craziness 'cause you got no control.

So, what am I supposed to do, *genius*?

He stared at you, checking to see if you were on the up and up, really wanted to know. He sat down again, looked around to make sure no one was listening, and whispered to you about this special clinic in the DR. He explained it was therapy, a few drugs, some counseling, and you wouldn't be the sucio you are now. You'd have a normal life, like the one you want. You could approach your lady with a new attitude, because as soon as she saw you, she'd know you changed.

He ripped a corner off the newspaper and wrote something on it. Here, he said, handing it to you. Just ask for Viktor. He'll arrange everything. It works, dude, believe me, I know.

You thought about it hard but were in such bad shape you didn't have the energy to get on no plane. You bought The Writer's books and the sucios in his stories depressed you. You had met those dudes before. They were family members, past and present. They were you. Not one was happy, and you wanted to be happy. Deserved to be happy. If anything, The Writer knew sucios.

Days passed with you parked across the hospital trying to catch a glimpse of Sari. You sat there for hours to check if a guy picked her up, and no one did. You wondered if maybe she was a little lonely too. The Writer's words kept playing in your head. *Therapy, a few drugs, some counseling.*

Months later, you just had a lot of moping and hoping but no Sari. Nothing would have happened unless your uncle Justo told you he was going down to the DR on one of his revolving trips down there. He asked if you wanted to hang. You knew he was using you as cover for his wife, who for some stupid reason believed tio wanted to show you the patria before you became too gringof-ied. She had seen you grow up and always thought you were a pari-guayo. She thought with you around he wouldn't have time to get into trouble, but he was going down to see his Dominican honey. You had the blues bad, and this was your chance.

You called Viktor, and he gave you the rundown. Call "Viktor Dos" when you arrive at the hotel in Santo Domingo, Viktor Uno said. With American cash up front, no refunds. You should have known right there, but you were too blinded by love, so desperate, your New York BS Detector shut down. Besides, this was business as usual in the DR. You withdrew the money you were saving for that '68 cherry red GTO, packed and waited for your uncle.

Just like Viktor Uno had said, at the hotel they picked you up in a black SUV. You told tio you were visiting friends for a few days. His DR babe kept him busy, so he didn't even hear what you said. Two guys in the car, both wearing Ray-Bans, dressed in tight-fitting blue guayaberas. The one in the back, who looked like a Dominican sumo wrestler, fisted the money, counted it twice. Gotta blindfold you, he said, nothing personal. Then the car sped off.

You were on the road close to an hour. You know this because the radio DJs gave the time occasionally. It was a quiet ride. Bachata and merengue streaming from the radio, and air conditioning, the only noises in the car. They took you out, walked you into the facility, which smelled like Pine Sol and Vicks VapoRub. Walking through a hallway, you heard staff talking and laughing; otherwise, it was quiet. You rode up an elevator, a creaky metal gate closed and opened again after a laggy ride.

When they slid the blindfold off, you were sitting down and looking bleary-eyed at a gray-haired man with dark half-moons under his eyes, dressed in green scrubs. He held a cigarette between yellowed fingers, the smoke curling around him.

Hope you had a good trip, my friend. I'm Dr. Bengüey. I'm handling your case.

He flipped through papers in the long green folder, had you sign some forms. Everything looks in order. We'll start tomorrow. Now, they will show you to your room. He smiled, snapped his fingers and an orderly came and delivered you away to a chalk white room without windows. A fan with flickering bulbs hung from the ceiling.

You don't remember much after that, and if you did you would be trying to forget. They didn't even give you a chance to understand what had happened. You were groggy when they told you, like you were high on something crazy one of your boys copped from a dark corner in the Heights. You thought you saw a nurse who looked like Sari. They talked in Spanish which made it harder to understand. Something about equivocación. Más como un desvio fatal, someone whispered loud enough for everyone to hear. Laughter. Dr. Bengüey yelled at them, angry. Called them all kinds of names in Spanish. Half comatose, you kept saying you didn't understand.

That's what I get for working with idiotas, he said. He sat down next to you. You remember his eyes looking so sad you thought you might be dying.

Smiling, he told you everything happens for a reason.

Then, they got you up, blindfolded you again; rolled you out in a wheelchair. They forced those painkillers down your throat, made you feel loopy. Threw you back in the black SUV and dropped you at a city hospital. No one asked questions or answered yours.

The first time the nurses walked you to the bathroom, standing to pee, eyes closed, you searched but only grabbed air. The two nurses giggled as they sat you down. When you stood up, you caught a glimpse in the mirror and screamed. Mouth opened like you had seen a dead body, you shook and cried because it finally hit you.

They kept you there for weeks, gave you medication for the pain and to calm you down. Assigned you a shrink who said it was normal to be angry, but never talked about where to direct the anger. Those assholes made a big-ass mistake, and you asked her if she knew something. Your medical bills will be taken care of was all she said. Nobody knew anything, and you don't even know the location of the place. Couldn't remember enough details to tell any lawyer what happened. Just the thought of dealing with the Dominican authorities and legal system made you nauseous.

Forget about suing. Instead, she talked about acceptance and adapting, but you were hung up on what happened to your dick and balls. Did they at least give them a proper funeral? Or just toss them in the garbage? You placed your hand on your crotch, praying to God, promising to end your sucio ways, hoping that He would make them reappear, but all you felt was emptiness and loss.

Then came the dilation sessions. The nurses showed you how to do it the first few times. After that, you were on your own. You had to insert dildos into a hole your body never had. You didn't want to do it. Your body senses it as a wound, the doctor explained, so it will try to heal itself by closing it up. An impatient nurse took another approach. You have a vagina now, you need to take care of it, she scolded. That includes screwing yourself for life if you aren't getting laid, the snarky one piped in. After the laughter died down, the oldest one looked at you as she propped your pillow. Without missing a beat, she looked at you with motherly eyes. Welcome to womanhood, she said.

They released you, so you took your dilators and returned home. Your uncle didn't even blink when you got around to visiting. He figured you had found a honey of your own and left without you. Like many sucios, he didn't talk much, especially when watching a ballgame. He just sat there, enjoying the lazy buzz from the beer and summer day. He looked up once and threw a long glance at you. You look different, he said, you've lost weight. You wanted to tell him, because you needed to tell someone. He was your favorite tio, after all, and as sucios go more understanding than your father or brothers. But you recalled his jokes about mariquitas and pajaros, remembering the times you joined in with your own putdowns, and how you laughed along. You thought about your cousin Dianelys when she came out. Her religious parents' shame proved stronger than their love, so they threw her out of the house. She roamed the streets and settled into hopping from one friend's sofa to another. No one in the family stood up for her. Not you, not her aunt—your Puerto Rican mother—and definitely not tio Justo.

Your case would be scandalous, even viral worthy. They couldn't understand Dianelys, thought she was being faddish, rebellious. Una etapa, a stage, Titi Yari always says, before blaming her daughter's friends for brainwashing her. She's too pretty to be una bucha, she'd add. Y con ese cuerpazo? As if lesbians couldn't be pretty or voluptuous, like they're all butch. Imagine what they'd think of you. Un monstruo, a freak, that's what. There wasn't enough wrapping to wrap their heads around what happened to you. As they did with anything beyond their limited comprehension that offended their narrow sensibilities, they would react with fists. When you said goodbye to your uncle that day, you knew it would be the last time you saw him and the family. It was a preemptive strike. Why tell them and suffer in exile as the family's running joke? Fuck that, you said. With that, you walked out of your uncle's apartment and closed the door on your past life.

Truth is, though, you had no clue what the new life was supposed to be. You just wanted to bury the old one. You spent a lot of time with the new therapist trying to figure it out. Cavalo specialized in LGBTQ patients. At first, you were uncomfortable being thrown into that mix. You didn't feel gay or anything like that and you asked to get another therapist. Sure, I can try, Cavalo answered. But I don't know many regular practitioners who would take a case as unique as yours. Honestly, I don't think any therapist not specializing in this community can even begin to help you.

That made sense to you. Looking back, you wonder if early on Cavalo regretted taking your case. He demonstrated Job-like patience toward your sucio mentality trapped in a transitioned body. He listened to your angry rants, intervening only to recommend that you consider using less offensive language, or to suggest alternate ways of seeing things. He kept explaining that what you had learned about yourself as a man didn't jive with your new body. That what you had learned about being a man was something constructed, which you didn't understand. You kept telling him you weren't gay. Fine, he would say. Let me break it down to you this way: you have a vagina and cannot produce the hormone that makes you look like a man, but you see yourself as a specific type of man. And that's a recipe for cognitive dissonance.

He walked you through the options. There was reversal surgery. The breakdown didn't sound appealing. It was expensive, involved taking tissue from a thigh or forearm which left scarring. It required using a penile implant, and it simply wouldn't ever be the same. On top of that, you would need the hormone therapy, anyway. No, you couldn't go through another operation. Through the excruciating pain again. The first one was hard enough, and reversal required years of surgeries and money you didn't have. You googled the pics and that broke the deal.

Cavalo spelled it out for you. If you're attracted to women, you can find intimacy with them. If you want to continue presenting as a man, he said, we can continue the testosterone therapy. Continuing with testosterone therapy led you to believe you'd lead a life as a hairy lesbian. You imagined going to a bar, returning home, and undressing to screams. The idea seemed such a non-starter to you. It was like living a lie.

Well, you would have to be honest with your partner, Cavalo instructed.

Oh, yeah, that's gonna get me a ton of hits, doc.

Perhaps, you're focusing too much on what you lost.

What's the point of looking like a man if you can't even satisfy a woman as a man?

There are many ways to satisfy your partner, Amador.

Sounds like lots of fingering and licking without the payoff.

The therapist closed his eyes and took a deep breath. You have another idea, besides the surgery?

You did not.

Listen, he said, give it some time. You need to explore what will make you the most comfortable and the happiest.

You sure as hell weren't happy. But you weren't happy when you had your dick and balls either, face it. You weren't much of a sucio, and in moments of honest reflection you hated everything behind it. You flew down to DR because you thought being less of a sucio would make you happy. Sure, losing your favorite limb and accessories was not in the plan, but here you were, and the alternatives were limited. You knew, deep down, that you had to make the best of the situation.

Cavalo recommended you explore the new focal point of your sexual pleasure. You peeked at it with a mirror, like he suggested. Your first thought was how beautiful it was. Then, thankful that the doctor had done an amazing job. Had not butchered you in the process and left you bleeding to death somewhere. As you examined every inch of it, you stopped to recall a precise image of your penis but couldn't. The dilation wasn't a chore any longer. You lingered and learned to get aroused. Weeks later, your first orgasm shocked you, left you breathless, feeling satisfied and yet frightened.

You had a new crew now, along with a new cell, job, and apartment. A new routine, too, with visits to the clinic, group sessions, appointments with Cavalo, trips to the lawyer to legally change your name to Tiresia Fuentes. That was the first name of your grandmother, who people called La Bruja, because she could read the cards and tell fortunes. You wished she had told yours, but she never read the cards for family. It didn't matter anyway, because the future was here now and there was no turning back. You had started hormone therapy. As your body morphed itself into a woman's, you marveled at your breasts. After the facial electrolysis, your face glowed, and you looked forward to doing the rest of your body. It seemed weird at first, but you liked the smoothness and never having to shave every day. With the fade haircut and your clothing, the look was unmistakably butch.

At the clinic, the trans women had heard about your case through the grapevine. At first, no one spoke to you. They eyed you from a distance. A few just saw you as a cis male who had bad luck or got what you deserved, depending on perspective. One of them called you a freak show. As your transition blossomed in front of their eyes, and you struggled with issues they understood firsthand, some became more sympathetic. You listened to their advice and thanked them for their generosity. With these women, you couldn't hide your vulnerability. They had no patience for fronting. Not when they had been trying to free themselves from a lie they had been living all their lives. They knew your pain like no one else, and the smartest move you ever made was accepting that and just listening. The few who couldn't label you, they would always hate you. But you never felt close enough to make friends. You shared similar moments, but you knew your experience was nothing like theirs. You didn't feel like you could offer anything to them as a friend. Or that you could ever belong to their tribe. You were flying solo on this journey, whose destination now seemed as murky as the point of departure, and the only sure thing was the turbulence along the way.

In your mind, there remained snapshots, glimpses of your former self that only a mirror would suddenly crack. That, or the invasive stares. The rude questions about your gender. The pause when addressed as "sir." The aggression, anger, and disgust directed at you when some hetero called you a dyke. Before, your beatings came from an outraged husband or lover. Now, a threat could jump out of the shadows without provocation.

Like that time at the club. You were on the last hour of your shift, and this young suit kept calling you bulldykebitch. The place was jammed and maybe he wasn't getting his Jäger Bombs fast enough. Maybe he had a bad day at work and hadn't got laid in months. Whatever the reason, you were tired and didn't need to put up with his crap. You so wanted to smash his face, but you told Eric, the bouncer, to deal with him. Eric asked him to leave, but the dude wouldn't have it. The other patrons cheered and laughed when Eric grabbed him and threw him out.

On the way out, you stopped to throw out the garbage and he was by the dumpster smoking a cigarette. Was he waiting for you? You really don't know. But he caught you off guard. You were stunned that after the names he hurled at you with every punch, he tried to rape you. You jabbed his eyes and he staggered backward and fell. That's when you stomped him in the crotch. You picked up your messenger bag and ran toward the subway.

At home, you undressed and checked the bruises on your body and face. Your wrist ached. You put an ice bag on your cheek and lips, then your wrist. You were going to need makeup for the face. After a long, hot shower, you lit a blunt and put on Drake's *Take Care*. And you couldn't help it, but you cried. Was this it, you kept thinking. Was this your life forever? You speed dialed Cavalo. Luckily, he took the call. You blurted you weren't feeling good, had unhealthy thoughts running through your head. He kept you on the phone for more than an hour and calmed you down. Praised you for defending yourself and for your progress. That re-ignited your sobbing, and he told you to breathe. Then he made room for you in his schedule the next morning. Before hanging up, he said: Terri, I know a LGBQT Community Center that sponsors a self-defense class.

After class, she came over. This surprised you, more than her being there. In the warm-up session, she flipped a look your way. Her smile filled you with happiness. You thought there was some recognition, maybe a connection. When she approached you after class, and asked about your wrist, it was obvious she did not.

Hi, I'm Sari, she said. I'm not being nosy, I'm a nurse. You explained how you injured your wrist. She scanned your bruised face. Guess that's why you're here, huh, she said. You smiled and nodded.

Been there, girl, she added, and cupped your good hand. You should have that checked, though. And keep icing it. She smiled again and collected her stuff. She owned a fantastic smile, a revelation because you never saw it once back in the hospital. See you around, you said, and you both exchanged goodbyes. She looked super fine, perhaps more so in those yoga pants. Her abundant hair, now loose and curly, framed her face beautifully. Ain't this a bitch, you thought.

Back home you wondered why she didn't recognize you. Before showering, you checked yourself in the mirror. The breasts, of course, and your body was softer all around. You had gained a little weight. True, in some places more than others. Was your face that different? You still saw *you*, just with less hair. It had been a while, and how many patients does she see in the hospital every day? But the truth was that when you were there, she had not really seen you. All she saw was a sucio.

A few classes later, you went out for the proverbial cup of coffee. It became clear that you were both into each other. In a romantic comedy, this would be the moment for the montage of the couple doing fun stuff. Each clip suggesting a deeper, bonding relationship. Two people doing that magical thing with everything clicking. The chemicals of love reaching peak levels, a lot of kissing, eye gazing, holding hands and intertwining fingers, long phone calls, loss of hunger and sleepless nights. In your case, also having someone to visualize while dilating. Everything was wonderful.

Except for one major problem. What about when you finally decided to do it? You had not dated. Too much overtime to pay your couch time, you told Cavalo, but really you were afraid. You had never taken this new body for a test drive, and your mind had an obsolete handbook. It was like you were an old rookie, or better yet a foreign player in a new league. You'd hope when the moment came that you could bring your A game to a second sport in an arena you had never played in.

Despite all of that, this wasn't your biggest concern. The real problem was that she did not know about your past, and the secrecy gnawed at you. If you didn't tell her, you would suffer that lie for the rest of your lives, if it lasted that long. And what if one day something you said or did triggered that time in the hospital? Or she found out about your sucio ways some other way. You cut all contacts with everyone in your past, and sooner or later she would ask about your family. You feared meeting up with a relative or a friend within your old six degrees. What if she were with you when that happened? She'd be really pissed at your dishonesty. From history, you could assume this woman would not take that lightly. The more you ruminated, the more you knew it could only work if she knew. Even if she remembered you as a sucio. Even if the idea of what happened to you disgusted her. And you lost her, forever.

Yo, you were supposed to get some drugs, not get your dick hacked off.

That was The Writer talking, after you cornered him at his usual table in Starbucks. He didn't recognize you. He blinked at you as you seized him by the shirt, and he swore it wasn't his fault.

You had been sitting at the next table, listening to him spin his lies on a shapely young woman. Even after everything you experienced, when every single sucio cell in your brain, every sucio instinct in your body, had apparently vanished. Swish. Gone. You still knew The Writer was laying down moves on her right out of the Sucio Training Manual. And she was too naïve to catch on. He had played her. She confronted him and he had told her she should know better. That she was a grown woman and the drama was pathetic.

You the finest bitch in here, you know that, he told her. You rolled your eyes and shook your head as you scoped the place. Besides butchy you, an old lady gummed her muffin, the pimply barista was preparing a latte, and an emaciated teen with Medusa dreads seated across from a dwarf reading the newspaper, sipped water while texting. The Writer caressed her hand and stared long-ingly into her eyes. We had fun times, didn't we? That's all that matters, right?

You knew this strategy all too well. In his mind, it would end up with make-up sex, one last good lay, before he dumped her sculpted ass. Once you confront a sucio, he is searching for the exit, but he will always try to get one more lay before he does.

Maybe it wouldn't have bothered you if this morning Sari hadn't told you: Too much to process, I need time to think about us. She had stayed over another night and your love making left you feeling too clean and pure to keep lying. After making her breakfast, you broke it down. At first, she stared at you, eyes circling your face to find the sucio buried in you. Then, exasperated, she said, I cannot connect that person with you, Terri. But the lying, she added, shak-ing her head, standing to leave.

You begged for forgiveness for not telling her sooner. For being that asshole who set in motion her rejection and everything else that followed. Sari was a good woman who had been burned once too often and her level of trust was at an all-time low. You did right in telling her, but history is a bitch, especially when it repeats itself. She left the door cracked, but you knew it could close at the last minute, for good.

So, you had no time for what The Writer was pulling. And your patience had run out. You stood up and turned to the young wom-an. Get out, you yelled.

Whoa, who you talking to like that, dude. He stood up, fronting like he does.

That's when you grabbed him by the shirt.

Get out, you repeated, and she pranced out the door in her stilettos.

Do I have to call the cops? the barista yelled.

You shoved the little rat back into his chair. Nah, we good.

You smiled at him. Then you brought him up to speed. That's when he apologized, said it wasn't his fault.

You just stood there. If you had met him right after the surgery, you might seriously have killed him. Or hurt him real bad. That seemed so long ago, when you were someone else. Someone barely recognizable, memorable. Someone who took a detour and arrived somewhere better.

You grabbed your bag.

You know what, writer man, you said, nodding. I want to thank you. Really.

Then you put your shades on and walked into a gorgeous, bright New York afternoon.

THE OPERATION

ONLY TWO YEARS AGO, Elena had worn the blue dress for her wedding, having sewn it herself from flowery fabric her mother gave her. Now, the unzipped dress draped her slender body, as she sat on the bed caressing the faded sheet where they had created their two children, who slept on rags spread across the floor. She got up and glanced around the home Facundo had built, another shack crowding the marshes in El Fanguito. The ten-by-twelve wooden box had enough room for the cot, a small table, two chairs and a rattan chair reserved for guests. Facundo had put up a drop-down shelf where she could prepare food, and she cooked over firewood near an open window. The splintered, gray wooden walls held two pictures: Jesus on the Cross and the stern face of Pope Pius XII. She straightened the pile of books stacked in a corner, relics from a time she dreamed of becoming a teacher, before her father took her out of school and told her she needed to work and help the family.

She opened the shutters and looked out toward the bay. Facundo used to say all these shacks had the look of hope, because they were temporary, and everyone aspired to something better. Seeing the shining, cloudless day, it could feel that way. Later, after the smog from the garbage dump settled across the bay, and the putrid smell from the surrounding water crept into their nostrils, the weather-beaten shanties just represented misery.

She spotted Lola, her neighbor and friend across from her, preparing breakfast.

Lola, remember to keep an eye on Carmencita and Fredie, she yelled. Lola nodded, while frying eggs. Sure, bring them over.

Elena knelt by her children. The girl breathed, burdened with congestion; the boy swatted at a fly buzzing around his head. Their faces made her stop and stare. She started to cry but quickly brushed away the tears and woke them up. She nudged Carmencita toward Lola's shack and carried Fredie. There, they plopped on the bed, along with Lola's two children. Lola's husband Pucho had already left for work at the textile factory where Facundo had worked. They used to leave together. Facundo always kissed her goodbye and a few feet away would turn to smile and wave. The last time, the smile came across as curt and the wave, an absent-minded gesture. That evening Pucho informed her that Facundo's arm got caught in the carding machine and ripped it off. When they finally arrived at the hospital he had already died.

Lola zipped up Elena's dress and offered her a chunk of bread and coffee. You can't go off without eating, she said. Elena had little appetite. Her stomach groaned more from nervousness than hunger. She tore off pieces of bread and dunked them in the coffee. After eating, she kissed her sleeping children, said goodbye to Lola and ran back to her shack to find her only pair of shoes. It was a mile-and-a-half to the hospital and she rarely wore shoes.

From her house Elena crossed filthy water walking on wooden planks mounted on cement blocks. Along the way, she waved to women cooking, scrubbing clothes on washboards or pinning them on lines; passed old men inhaling cigarette butts and drinking coffee, or chewing tobacco as they swung on hammocks; children playing barefoot and naked on the debris piled around the shacks. Two boys played in a wrecked rowboat in the shallow marshes.

A heavyset woman carried a large tin can of water. Scraggly dogs snarled and barked. A little man plucked a guitar and sang "Lamento Borincano." He smiled and winked at her. Elena looked down and kept walking.

Past the borders of the slums, she connected to the city's network of paved streets and sidewalks. She passed buildings, cars, and buses. The cement buildings offered shadowy relief from the rising sun. Elena shrunk from the stares of people walking by. They knew she was from El Fanguito, even with her fancy blue dress and too-tight shoes. Her aching feet pushed her on, down Calle Labra toward Magdalena.

At the corner, she asked a woman where the hospital was. The woman pointed and told her a few more blocks. She wanted to rest but didn't want to arrive late and miss her opportunity. The women in her barrio had told her to get there early and certainly before noon when everyone would go on a long lunch break.

You're so lucky to take Facundo's place, Lola told her. The foreman likes you, that's why, she said with a laugh. Elena didn't appreciate the joke. She missed Facundo but was happy and fortunate that the supervisor took pity on her.

Facu was a great worker. It's the least I can do, he said. But you need the certificate. Can't hire you without that paper, he warned.

He meant the certificate from the hospital. At first, she was scared. Amalia Ortiz said it wasn't so bad. It was like a little vacation. A little pain, but it goes away after a few days, Amalia said. Others told her they put you to sleep. What if you didn't wake up? But these thoughts meant nothing. Without a job what would she do? She needed to feed her children. She couldn't sew like in the old days and make money. The factories had taken those jobs, and the stream of seamstress work was drying up. Working at the textiles was better than taking a few dollars from spotty work.

This was the same hospital where she had to identify Facu's corpse. In the morgue, down below. They didn't notify her, but instead let Pucho do it hours after his death. It was the first time she had ever been to a hospital. First time she ever saw a dead body.

She doesn't know why she didn't cry. Perhaps she had cried herself out of tears, or maybe it felt so much like a dream that the body on the gurney didn't seem like her husband's. When they asked her to confirm his identity, it snapped her out of the dream, and she noticed they had cleaned him of any blood and covered the stump. She nodded and they whisked her out of the room.

The waiting room was stark white like the morgue, but much warmer. Instead of dead bodies, it was full of women dressed in flowery dresses and uncomfortable shoes. Some had their hair done for the doctor's visit. A few assistants were helping women with paperwork. A woman wearing cat-eyed glasses behind a desk told her to sit and someone would help her fill out the many forms. Elena told her she could read and write. Surprised, the woman gave her a pen, and told her to leave anything she could not answer or understand. It was getting warmer and the ceiling fans kept whipping hot air. The women in the room were young, in their twenties or thirties. One or two in their mid to late thirties. Elena had turned eighteen two weeks earlier. She had two young children and no miscarriages. She wrote that down. Healthy, as far as she knew. Widow.

There was no line on the form that could hold the pain she felt losing her husband so young. A good, hard-working man, who loved his wife and children. No questions asking about the loneliness greeting her every daybreak. No place to write down how she missed her family she left in Villalba when they moved to the capital after the Herminia Sugar Plantation closed and Facundo lost his job. Everyone said the jobs were in San Juan now, working inside factories rather than outside under the sun like beasts of burden. What difference does it make, Facundo used to say, if inside it was hotter than hell.

A nurse called her name. She took her vitals, checked her eyes, throat, and ears; then, escorted Elena down a white hall with many offices. She opened the door into one and with the large green folder signaled Elena to enter. The nurse handed the folder to the doctor, a wavy-haired man behind a desk, wearing a stiff white lab coat over a white shirt and skinny blue tie.

The doctor appeared fond of the beach. His face had a ruddy shine and with his watch laying on his desk, Elena saw he was normally quite pale. He motioned her to sit. The room had nothing on the walls but the doctor's diplomas. On his large desk, piled with green folders, a name plate introduced him: Daniel H. Stieve. He did not look up from the papers in the folder. His blue eyes narrowed as he crouched over the papers, nodding his head, ruffling them with elegant, tapered fingers, at one point scratching a curving eyebrow with the back of a thumb. In Spanish, he asked if she had two children.

Yes, Elena responded. Carmen and Fredes. It's all there. He looked up. His thin lips forced a smile.

And you're here for the operation, yes?

Elena nodded, gulping, unable to pronounce the word "yes."

Are you sure, Mrs. Fonseca?

I need a job ... and they need the certificate, Doctor.

He closed the folder and sat back, and really looked at her for the first time. How young she was, he thought. How sad, too, the pretty dress so loose on her thin body. They always came with the only decent article of clothing they owned. This woman did not have her hair done like others. Her lustrous hair, free and unfettered, suited her, cradling her angular face and serious brown eyes, which now looked straight at him.

Have you discussed this with your husband?

If my husband were alive, doctor, I would not be here.

He nodded. I see. He rang a bell for the nurse.

Nurse Estrada, please give Mrs. Fonseca all the information she needs to prepare her for surgery.

Isn't it today?

The doctor and nurse looked at each other. Smiled at her.

Oh no, you need to come back at a scheduled time, early in the morning and follow the nurse's instructions.

The nurse explained everything to her. How she needed to fast and arrive at another section of the hospital a week later at eight in the morning. That it was a long procedure. She had known about staying at the hospital, but now she needed to bring clothes, stay later than she imagined. She hoped Lola could take care of the children for those few days. They said complications could occur. Luisa Santiago had died from complications. What if she died? Who would take care of Carmencita and Fredie? The thought of both of them orphans almost made her faint. But what could she do, alone and without a job? She could not return to Villalba and become a burden for her parents, who had younger siblings in their cramped house.

She sat on a bench and slipped off her shoes. She thought about the people in jackets and beautiful clothes driving nice cars. What must it be like not to worry where your next meal will come from? To not worry a hurricane will leave you homeless. How comforting to know your children will grow up healthy and live to have children of their own. That maybe they will get an education and become something. That you'll live to see grandchildren.

A woman dressed in a linen dress and hat crossed the street, tightly holding the hands of two little girls wearing summer dresses, their hair in braids. They laughed as they skipped across in their patent leather Mary Janes. The oldest wanted sesame candy from a vendor's cart parked by the curb. The youngest started chanting for a coconut one. The mother opened her purse and took out some change. They jumped, screaming out their flavors, as the man opened the glass door to retrieve the treats.

Elena sighed, slowly put on her shoes, and headed back to El Fanguito.

She had been one of many patients, but he couldn't get her out of his mind. It wasn't her youth alone that unnerved him. Most of the women were young. Their hard lives had molded them into older women before they had a chance to live their youth. She was at that point where she was holding on to the vestiges of youthful vigor and spark. That loose dress struck him as sad. It seemed an afterthought, like her childhood and whatever she had of her adolescent years. Her problems were already defining her thin body, her face.

His youngest sister Emily was only two years older. Her most stressful concerns were choosing a dress to wear for an important event or the marriageability of the current beau. Elena Fonseca wore worry better than her lovely flowery dress. And yet, her presence bore a certain self-assurance and pride that gave him immediate respect for her. What did a smile look like on her lips? If she had had anything to smile about, he might know.

Often after his shift, Daniel Stieve walked to Punta Piedrita and sat by the beach to smoke a cigarette. As he squinted toward the ocean, the setting sun warming his face, he wondered how anyone could not smile every day in this tropical paradise. He had visited El Fanguito, too, several times, on house visits or to promote the program. The residents gave you the biggest plate of food, or the best seat in the house, when they had so little to offer. Lovely people, really, he thought. What a shame there's so much poverty.

Right out of medical school Daniel Stieve joined the Army Medical Corps and served in the Pacific during the war. After the war, he was stationed in the Philippines and later in Hawaii. While others complained of tropical life and climate, he loved it. When he learned about this position in Puerto Rico working with the Rockford Institute, he snapped at it. Anything to get as far away as possible from Georgia. His father disapproved, of course. You're wasting your career in the jungles, he said. An established and renowned pathologist, his father had achieved professional success and thought he knew what was best for anyone else in the field. As usual, he never considered another person's uniqueness or personality, or even his dreams. What's a dream to someone who spent so much time studying death? Daniel was the oldest and naturally carried the burden of his father's legacy. That legacy was not the only issue.

When his father married his mother, a non-Jewish woman, a shiksa, he not only severed ties with his family but also a religion, a culture, and thousand years of history. In moments when he allowed himself pride in his Jewishness, his father would often claim "We're like diamonds. The more pressure on us, the more we shine.

Look what we've contributed to the world." He kept that to himself, though. They lived in the Deep South, among Baptists and snake-holding, tongues-speaking Evangelicals, the KKK and burning crosses. His father buried his religion, his ethnicity, claimed that in the long run it didn't matter, a furtive way to acknowledge his agnosticism. Perhaps because he was a man of science, he held a different perspective on life and the world.

Serving in the Pacific spared Daniel from marching into the camps. From confronting the striped specters at the gates who pointed with shriveled blue-dotted arms toward the mass graves. Other visions would fuel his nightmares, but not those. Back home, he saw the photos and news reels, met survivors, even a soldier from the 42nd who liberated Dachau. When Daniel approached the subject with him, his father said, We've been persecuted for millennia—does it surprise you?

It was then Daniel realized how far his father had drifted from his Jewish roots, and consequently had pushed him and his siblings even further away. His mother, the former Mary Ellen Simpson, a bona fide Southern belle with ancestry that featured slaveowners who fought for the Confederacy, and at least one Klan Grand Dragon, was embarrassed by her family. It made sense that his parents were attracted to each other. When it came to Jewish matters, his mother had absolutely no clue, and she never made it a point to guide Daniel toward that part of his ancestry. She was Episcopalian and by Southern standards a liberal. She accepted her husband's lack of religious belief, chalked it up to his "scientific mind." She never attempted to convert him. Never even broached the topic when he proposed, and they married at the local courthouse. She attended services during holidays, and the children's introduction to religious instruction was decidedly Christian by default. She never tired of commenting that by Judaic law he and his siblings were not Jewish. Between his father's agnosticism and his mother's lax faith, he slipped into a spiritual void he never questioned.

When he arrived at Presbyterian Hospital, he thought it would be like any other fellowship and residency in obstetrics. In a way, it was. He treated patients, delivered babies, and performed related surgical procedures. Early on, his superiors informed him about the program, but he didn't realize the resources behind it and the importance the hospital gave it. He spent more time performing tubal ligations and hysterectomies, but he didn't think much of it. In his third year, one of the new residents, Malcolm Parnell, quit after only a few months. By then an attending physician, he asked Parnell why he was leaving. I don't like what's going on here, he said, agitated. His response surprised Daniel, irked him.

It's a method to better plan families, he said, puzzled.

Parnell shook his head, smiled. Look, Dr. Stieve, it just doesn't sit right with me, and I don't want to waste the Institute's time and money. At the door, head down, he turned around and said: There's more to this program than you think, sir.

Perhaps Parnell's comment alluded to rumors about the infamous letter written by one of the founding members of the Institute, who had worked at the hospital. Dr. Cornell Robb allegedly 45 wrote a letter to a friend in which he called Puerto Ricans "dirty animals" and supposedly stated he was trying his best to exterminate as many as he could. That was the story circulating around, but nothing was verified. Those who knew Robb and defended him called the allegations preposterous and outrageous. They referred to his peculiar sense of humor which might have given others a false impression of a man who possessed a sterling record of achievement. What they did at the hospital was known to all, even supported by local government, which had passed Law 116 in favor of population control initiatives. True, the Institute had earned a reputation for developing an air of secrecy, but that was typically the case with many programs undergoing research.

Parnell probably had never seen El Fanguito, the squalor and suffering, he thought. The more he thought about the young man's righteous arrogance, the more relieved he was that he had left. This was not work for the faint of heart, he thought.

His fiancée, Magda, a native, agreed and supported him. Stop worrying about what others think, she told him. The poor here are ignorant and need a little push sometimes, she said. Her father's workers always wanted higher wages, she complained, because their families kept growing. If they stopped having kids and spending their pay on booze and gambling, they'd have enough.

Elena arrived at the hospital early, wearing the blue dress and tight shoes. This time, she carried a suitcase with clothing, toiletries, a copy of *La Charca*, and a wrinkly photo. The black-and-white photo was in a traditional pose those days: she, Facu, and the children, standing next to a long vertical, wooden stand with the word "Recuerdos" painted on the side. They had taken it during the fiestas patronales. It was the only picture she had of them. The suitcase was a communal one. It had gone from one barrio woman to another as they visited the hospital for the operation. She had left Fredie and Carmencita with Lola, who couldn't hide her tears after she kissed them goodbye, which upset her.

The walk to the hospital was the loneliest of her young life. Near daybreak, the city had not yet broken into its rhythm. Streets held a calming stillness that frightened her. How strange, she thought; dressed up and carrying a suitcase but not really going anywhere. Her stomach grumbled from fasting, and she just wanted to get it done. And return to the children, she hoped. She crossed herself. Prayed to God to see her through the operation safely.

In the morning, after they prepped her, she lay in bed. Doctor, the tubes, she asked, they can untie them, yes? He held a clipboard tightly in his hands.

What do you mean?

I can have children—later?

The doctor paused, looked down, then smiled at her with sparkling white teeth. Well, Mrs. Fonseca—that's in God's hands, is it not?

She nodded and lay back her head on the pillow. The doctor shook his head. For some reason, patients had this idea that Fallopian tubes could be opened and closed like faucets. This untying business was the bit of misinformation disseminated from one woman to another, like some home remedy or handed-down folk wisdom. Even after explaining the procedure as a way of preventing pregnancies, this is what they wanted to hear. The hospital didn't want to alarm women at this stage of the procedure. One had to balance the benefits of the operation, which patients had consented to undergo for a variety of practical reasons, with the fear and anxiety they normally experienced before surgery.

They put her in a wheelchair and rolled her to the operating room. As they lay her on the table, and applied anesthesia, she thought, Dear God, if you take me, please take care of my children.

On the table, with her gaunt face, she looked more like one of his father's patients, Stieve thought. Yet she had a pretty face, and her skin was radiant and healthy. The OR was respectfully still. The nurse, anesthesiologist, and three male residents waited for his instructions. With scalpel in hand, he scanned the exposed shaven pubic area, with the other hand smoothed it out.

This is an eighteen-year-old woman, two children, no history of spontaneous abortions. Her vitals are all excellent, and she presents <u>47</u> a good affect prior operation. He cut into skin and muscle, opening her up.

Today we're performing a bilateral partial salpingectomy, using the Pomeroy Technique. The nurse wiped his brow. A simple and effective procedure, he said, inserting his fingers into the incision.

Identifying the fallopian tube, making sure I have it. The nurse slapped a clamp into his hand. Then clamp it with a Babcock on the proximal portion of the ampulla, like this … You now elevate the tube, thus, and expose the vascular supply of the mesosalpinx. Do you all see? The nurse hydrated the area. The three residents bent forward for a view and nodded. Everything looks good here—healthy–she could have had many more babies.

He groped the organ with his fingers. It's imperative that you distally follow the path of the tube to its fimbriated end, so as not to mistake it for the round ligament. Understand? More nods. Now, using a strand of suture, tie the knuckle of tube tightly. He grabbed another clamp from the nurse. Replace the Babcock with the Hemostat to proceed to the next step. He wrapped another strand of suture around the loop of tube and the nurse handed him a pair of scissors. Pulling the clamp, he cut into the tube.

Keep traction at a minimum as you pierce the mesosalpinx and excise one centimeter of tube with the Metzenbaum. The nurse grabbed the piece of tube and tossed it in a pan. We'll be sending that to pathology. Pro forma.

His blue eyes glared between green scrub cap and mask. They pierced through the air toward one of the residents. Saunders, next step. The young man straightened up. Examine proximal and distal ends of the ligated oviduct for bleeding, sir. Stieve smiled. Excellent. The nurse hydrated again, and the doctor reviewed the area carefully, then returned the tube to the abdominal cavity. Fine, then, he said, round two.

After the operation, the Plant Manager told her to report in three weeks for work. We all liked Facu and understand your situation, but we can't hold it forever, he said. Plenty of men needing work.

She reported, sore, her stitches bandaged. A bottle of iodine and fresh bandages in her purse. Fresh underwear, too, in case blood seeped through the bandages. Standing for hours was bad enough, but she also had to cart the rolls of lap to her machine because the men who rolled them refused to do it. Pucho would lift the heavy rolls into the machine for her. He received a lot of angry stares and remarks from the other men, but she knew he would get worse from Lola if he didn't. Their taunts and derision were unable to detain her quick hands and agile fingers. Her tenacity impressed the men, although they would never admit it. Eventually, they had to accept her, if not respect her.

She arrived home, legs and arms bunched in knots, her back aching. The whirling of the machines stuck in her ears. At home, with flecks of cotton spotting her dress and hair, she started dinner—usually taro, yucca with codfish or rice and beans, sometimes chicken. Or just a fried egg over rice. After dinner, she visited Lola for a cup of coffee and the latest gossip.

She reveled in the intimate moments with her children. Brushing Carmencita's hair or teaching Fredie how to read became pleasurable, precious rituals. When they slept, she stole a few minutes for herself, to sew while listening to the radio. Other times, she read by the kerosene lamp, falling asleep a few pages into the book. Many times, her thoughts turned to Facu, the warmth of his rough hand caressing her cheek, the strong hairy chest that cushioned her weary head, his silly jokes. Mostly, she missed his voice whose absence made her loneliness so tangible and real.

As Carmencita and Fredie got older they became needier. Fredie kept to himself. He found ways to entertain himself. Empty match boxes became miniature cars or building blocks. He would stay in Lola's house. When he started school, he would go straight to Lola's until Elena came home. He had not yet gotten that itch that made neighborhood children wander through the barrio. At home, he stayed close to his mother, hungry for her attention.

Carmencita was another matter. Lola kept complaining she could not control her. Salvaje, she called her. Wild. Without a word, she drifted out of the house, bored, and walked around the neighborhood. She didn't always come straight to Lola's after school. Doña Trina spotted her smoking cigarettes and kissing boys. The barrio women talked about how Elena had mourned long enough. She was pretty and young, but they joked "it" was going to dry out if she didn't find a man soon. More seriously, they would tell her to find a husband who could take her job, so she could be a better mother.

If there had been a single decent man in sight, maybe she would have considered the idea. All the men at the plant were married, and she wasn't the type to break a home. Neither was she the type to settle for a man she could not respect or who didn't respect her. The plant paid better than most jobs. She had money to buy food, clothing, and save for the future. She had worked hard to keep this job. She was good at it, and she didn't want to relinquish it to any undeserving man who probably would spend the pay on drink and cigarettes. The idea that she would have to beg money for underwear bothered her. Besides that, most men would not want to raise another man's children, and if they wanted children, she would have to have another operation. To go through that again the man would have to be special, and El Fanguito lacked that breed of man. As years passed, she resigned to being what everyone called her at the plant and barrio, la viuda, the widow.

The problems with Carmencita worsened as she entered adolescence. Elena pleaded with her to help around the house. She talked back to her for any little reason. Lola said she was disrespectful to her, too. On her way back from work, Elena found her in school uniform, sharing a cigarette with a boy a few years older. She was laughing, throwing her head back and tossing her hair, slapping his arm playfully. Suddenly, she saw that her daughter needed a bra. Her face flushed as she realized that she had not yet talked to her about menstruation.

Elena stood, hands on hips, waiting for Carmencita to catch her glaring gaze. But the daughter looked away as if she didn't know her own mother. Elena marched over to her. Carmencita held her ground, head and chin lifted, to stare back at her. What? she asked. For a second, Elena did not see the child who had come from her womb, but another barrio woman with threatening and defiant eyes. Elena slapped her and grabbed her hair. The young girl screamed and swatted her mother's arm as she pulled her toward home. Stay away from my daughter or I'll complain to the police, she told the boy. He laughed and blew Carmencita a kiss.

This better be the last time I come tired from work and find you whoring around. The girl sat at the little kitchen table, pouting, and staring out the window.

All I ask is that you look after Fredie. Prepare dinner. You want to be a woman? That's being a woman.

Carmencita smirked. Like you?

What's that supposed to mean?

You work a man's job and you ain't like the other moms. Everybody says so.

Elena sighed and sat down. She looked at her daughter, who stared back, nostrils flaring, eyes holding an emotion between anger and disgust.

Well, *everybody* don't buy the food you eat.

The girl sucked her teeth and went to sleep on the rags. Fredie was sitting on the bed crying.

On a hot and humid day, Elena came home to a sobbing Lola. She braced herself for another fight with her daughter, but her friend's sorry look startled her, made her grab for a chair. Lola just pointed to the bed, and Elena turned to the covered body.

Lola and some neighbors had brought Fredie into the ER already dead, expecting miracles. Dr. Stieve was on call during the shift when they carried his limp body to the emergency room. The boy drowned in the bay. He rarely left the house, Lola explained, but his sister had left with a young boy and he followed them. It was a hot day and they must have gone for a swim. The sister had disappeared. All the medical staff could do was cover the body and declare the boy dead. They told Lola to take the body home and contact the parent.

The funeral was short and simple. Dressed in black, the color she wore since Facu's death many years ago, Elena cried alongside the small wooden casket. Usually, any death, especially of a child, would bring out many from El Fanguito in support. But only a few friends attended. Her family lived too far, and her daughter had disappeared.

Dr. Stieve wanted to approach Elena and offer his condolences but thought it best to defer. From a distance, he wondered how he could have consoled her, at a moment when a child had died, and the other had run away. How could he look at her big brown eyes buried in grief and offer soothing platitudes to calm her? The question she dared ask years ago gnawed at his brain. In need of desperate reassurance, she might ask him again. And he would have deflected the question again. Only a monster would have told the truth.

HAWAII IS WHERE CO-
QUIS GO TO DIE

FROGS. TREE FROGS NO bigger than a quarter. That's
what had her driving down Hana Highway heading to Maliko
Bay. It was nighttime and Halia Sabatier wished she were home,
comfortable in her Muumuu, watching television, reading, or
baking. Instead, here she was, hunched over the steering wheel,
white-knuckling it, and squinting at the invading darkness. Driving at a pace that validated her O.L.D driver's license. Old Lady
Driver. That's what her ex-husband Ray called it. Well, I *am* old, she
thought. A few years from retirement, in fact, and HDOA had her
running around Maui killing teeny frogs.

They were small and harmless to humans, but the Department of Agriculture considered *Eleutherodactylus Coqui* an invasive species. Native to Puerto Rico, somehow a few hitched a
ride on a plant transported from there in the 1980s. One female
lays around 1,400 eggs a year. So, decades later, by the time government agencies took action, every island in Hawaii had Coqui
sightings—more like "hearings," because they hide behind leaves

and are hard to spot. The male's mating call, the repetitive ko-kee that gives it its name, reaches eighty decibels. A relentless chorus of horny male frogs yearning for a mate can drive anyone loony.

Halia turned the jeep onto a service road that curved down to the bay's coast. At the site, the crew had set up two tank trucks parallel to the bushes and trees. Workers sprayed the foliage with a mix of water and citric acid, using heavy high-pressure hoses. It was a perfect night for this work: crescent moon and it had rained all morning. Lou Ezura, the site supervisor, was helping a worker strap on a backpack sprayer. Halia shoved a headlamp down her Lauhala hat and headed his way. When Lou saw her walking toward him, stiff with hands by her side, chest outward, he knew something was up. Halia hardly ever came down to the sites.

The coquis' shrill chirping punctuated the night air. The sound wasn't so bad meters away, but closer it got noisy. Hawaiians complained about losing sleep. Businesses worried the incessant cacophony would hurt tourism. The sound was worse than jet planes and lawn mowers. Without predators, thousands of hungry coquis could wipe out endangered invertebrate native species, putting at risk an already fragile ecosystem. The state government feared infestation of agriculture. People just wanted the noise to go away.

Can't believe we're back here again, she said, scoping the area.

Yeah, I thought for sure we had them last time.

Last time was by the gulch, Lou. Now, here they are by the bay. Everyone's panicked they'll migrate south to agri areas.

We're making headway here.

'Ae, I know. But we're behind schedule and HDOA's up my ass. HISC members are going crazy.

Can you get us another truck?

She sighed. Three men wearing backpack sprayers chopped at the thick brush with machetes.

One might be freeing up over in Napili. I'll try but can't promise anything. I'm sending you more people, for sure.

She talked to the sprayers and other workers for a few minutes and drank the coffee Lou offered. After saying goodbye, she headed back to the jeep.

Have a great weekend, Lou yelled after her. Halia tilted a raised arm backward to wave.   So much effort and resources spent killing these frogs. She shook her head while starting the jeep. *Everyone's gone damn lolo.* Throughout the islands, neighborhood vigilante groups scoured suspected areas and burned the amphibian invaders with acid or hydrated lime. Tried freezing or cooking them. On the Big Island, schools trained students how to capture and kill the frogs. Hardware stores kept selling out on citric acid or materials needed to make traps. Higher-ups demanded results. Total annihilation. But do it with the resources you have. In the time they told her that over the phone, hundreds of eggs had hatched. As she drove down the highway back home, she took some deep breaths and exhaled.

Next morning found her in a more relaxing situation. Simple things like grating green bananas calmed her. Cooking distracted her from the pressures of work. She rarely made pastele stew. It was a lot of work. But Halia was in her parents' vacant house, seven months after scattering her mother's ashes into the ocean. Her sister Alana was meeting her there to discuss the sale of the house and the family plant nursery business. It seemed right to cook pastele stew, a recipe passed down from her paternal grandfather.

Angel Sabatier came to Hawaii a boy. When he turned 17, they handed him a machete and sent him to work in the cane fields. The family had lost everything in Puerto Rico when Hurricane San Ciriaco ravaged the island in 1899. With no other alternative, they boarded a steamship headed to promised work in an unknown, faraway place.

A century later, Halia was preparing a meal her father, Kaleo, taught her to make when she was thirteen. She doesn't know the history behind it. How the miles and geography transformed the tamales-like pasteles her Puerto Rican ancestors used to eat at Christmas into a stew. She just remembers her father's calloused fingers peeling green bananas, like his father had taught him before. Grating them fast without ever scraping his knuckles, which she always did. She just knew it was a tasty dish whose smell reminded her of good times in this house.

She had finished setting the table when Alana's food truck drove into the driveway. Her sister was coming from Waiehu Beach Park, where she sold fast food, beverages, and shaved ice to beach goers. You couldn't miss it. Her sister had drawn a colorful Hawaiian sunrise on the truck's side with "Alana's Grindz" in big letters over it. Alana jumped off the truck and hurried into the house carrying grocery bags. She always seemed in a hurry, walking while looking around like she had dropped something.

Got some sweet bread, she said, holding up the bags, breaking into her impish smile.

You're too good, sis. They hugged and air kissed. Although they lived thirty minutes apart, this was only the second time they had seen each other since the funeral. Halia wished she could blame it on their hectic lives, but it went deeper than that. Their distance had something to do with their six-year age gap. She understood that, accepted responsibility for not reaching out to her younger sister, especially during Alana's rebellious years. When she ran off to L.A. with a glam rock group and the years in rehab that followed.

They sat down to eat, devouring the stew, and cleaning the bowls with the last of the bread. Halia loved the stew with red wine, but she never served alcohol with her sister around. As they ate, they caught up, discussing the little that had changed. Halia complained about her job and wanting to retire. They caught up on each other's children and exes. Alana talked about her latest love interest, yet another blonde surfer.

What do you expect, she said, I'm at the beach most of the day. All the surfers blond?

Shut up, she laughed. At least, I'm not living a nun existence, as in getting none.

After cleaning up, Alana brought out the Fournier Brisca cards. They both agreed to put the business and house on the market and let the estate liquidator sell what they weren't keeping. They had a few items to divide among themselves. The division went smoothly, but as always there were things they both wanted. Some of their mother's jewelry, pieces that as far back as childhood both loved. It wasn't just about the jewelry. They both wanted a memento from their mother. So, they played Brisca for them, a game they learned from their dad.

Titi Marisol's Hawaiian bracelet went to Halia. The bracelet belonged to their only aunt, who died in a car accident after putting down her old, sick dog, Leroy—returning from the vet's, a drunk ran through a stop sign and slammed into her. She was only forty-three, single and without children. Their mom became the guardian of her sister-in-law's possessions, but never used any of the jewelry. And when it came to her own, she certainly didn't insinuate who should inherit what. Halia was happy to win. She had always loved the bracelet, a silver piece with Hawaiian flowers etched around it.

In a close game, Alana won the oval, gold earrings that belonged to her maternal great-grandmother, who brought them to Hawaii from southern Spain. Alana shrieked when she won and quickly put them on. She loved their intricate gold and beaded design. They're like flamenco earrings, she said, and stomped on the floor like a flamenco dancer. Halia liked them, too, but would never tell her sister she they looked better on her. Alana had always been the prettier one, lanky and athletic, the better dancer, the only one who would dare get tattoo sleeves. The earrings hung on her like exotic fruit, accentuating her bronzed face.

It got tougher with the next few items because they were sentimental, holding memories and more nostalgia than any object should have. Their mother's prized possession was a rosary, with a crucifix of Portuguese filigree design, that was in her family for centuries. When Jasmine's grandparents came from Portugal, her grandmother said it kept her safe on the long voyage. Halia's mother prayed with that rosary every night, at church, and at every Rosary she attended. She always put it away in its silver box and kissed the lid after closing it.

Her mother wrapped the rosary tight around her hands as if she were holding on to her mother after all those years. Halia wanted that, to keep her own mom close in the worst of times. Alana didn't attend many of those events or church for that matter. But the time she almost overdosed, her mother prayed for her, the rosary's beads digging into her tiny hands.

It went to Halia, as did the silver diamond earrings her father gave their mother on their thirtieth anniversary. One of many Alana missed because she was either in rehab or had disappeared or simply forgot. They were beautiful and looked great on her mom. If she had won them, she would have saved them for her daughter, for her wedding day. Halia was always the one with luck. Wasn't that the way—those who have keep getting, and the rest keep getting screwed.

Her opening hand for the next game didn't bode well. And this was the big one. Her dad's machete. The one their great-grandfather had brought to Hawaii. He was a cane cutter, and it was his prized moneymaker. After he bought a new one, he gave it to their grandfather Angel when he started working in the cane fields. Angel quit to start the nursery business, so he polished the machete and mounted it on the office wall.

When their father Kaleo inherited the business from Angel, he refurbished the machete and mounted it inside a class case which he placed on a shelf. It was the only memento from their dad, an object that held mystery and memories. A slice of family history they didn't know much about. Kaleo wasn't a man set on accumulating possessions. He didn't own jewelry, not even a watch. Only his wedding ring, which they buried with him at his request. He didn't want a burial at sea, which displeased some of his more traditional Hawaiian relatives. I've worked with dirt all my life, he said. No problem being buried in it.

They both had their ups and downs with their father. He could be stubborn and old-fashioned, but they loved him unconditionally. He was a wonderful, doting dad who worked hard to provide for them. He counseled them but never reproached them for not taking his advice. At the rehab center, he told Alana, Baby girl, you're breaking my heart, tears rolling down his leathery, furrowed face. She turned to the mint-colored wall plastered with cheesy posters. Watching her dad cry shook her. If she could take it all back, the things she had done in her wild days. But her dad and mom were dead, and she didn't have a time machine.

When Halia took the last trick and won, Alana slapped the table.

Oh, come on, she yelled. Really?

Halia hadn't seen the anger building inside her sister. She thought Alana's outburst was playful poking.

I can't help it if you suck at Brisca.

Screw you, Halia. You're just lucky. Selfish and greedy like always. You get all the luck and everything else and still want the rest.

Halia looked at her sister, speechless for a few seconds.

Is that how you really see me, Alana?

Why can't you share? Why can't you just give a little?

Maybe it's because you always get what you want and never take care of it. Like with the pets mom and dad bought you? The clothing, jewelry, cars, or anything? And that goes double for boyfriends.

Oh, like you did so great with Ray.

Don't, she warned. Just don't.

The hell with this. You know what it means for me to have something, any little thing from dad. She was standing and crying now.

Halia closed her eyes and exhaled. We've been through this, Alana. She started picking up the cards. It's a family heirloom, and I just can't trust you with it. You'll probably end up hocking it.

You bitch. She took off the flamenco earrings and slammed them on the table. I don't need anything from you. Just sell everything and give me my share.

Come on, Alana. Don't be like that. You can have mom's earrings, okay?

Alana grabbed her purse and flew out the door. She sped away in her lunch truck, flipping the finger.

After Alana left, Halia opened a bottle of red and watched television until she started nodding on the sofa. In bed later, she couldn't sleep, the exchange with her sister running through her mind. Why was it like this between them? Her only sibling and at times it felt like they were strangers, more often like adversaries.

She would find patches of sleep in between turns but kept waking. The fight with Alana, the disorientation of sleeping in her parents' house after so many years, the stress thinking about her job, the list of things she had to do with her parents' belongings. Alana was supposed to sleep over and help. Like other times, she had bailed.

The thick darkness outside unnerved her. The house was near the nursery, in Waiehu, far from the dense developments, like the one where she lived in Kahului. Here, there was considerable space between houses. She got up, fixed herself a cup of chamomile, and headed to the garage, where stacked boxes waited for inspection. She and Alana were supposed to sort out the junk from anything they could salvage or sell. Most of this stuff Halia had never seen. One small box labeled "Hani" caught her attention. Hani was her grandmother's nickname, short for Leihani.

She opened the cardboard box and found a half-finished quilt stuffed inside. Under the quilt was a simple, medium-sized koa wood box. On top of the box were two books, *A Dictionary of the Hawaiian Language* and *The Massie Case*. Snuggled inside the box, Halia found a small black-and-white marbled composition notebook. When she opened it, newspaper clippings, letters, postcards, and a photograph cut from a newspaper tumbled out.

The dark, broad-shouldered young man in the photo stared back at her. Halia could not take her eyes off the photo. The eyes. Penetrating, questioning, yet plaintive, sad but defiant. He had a virile face, and she wondered who he was and why this photo was among her tutu Hani's belongings. Curious, she sorted the documents. All the clippings, from the *Advertiser* and *Star-Bulletin*, were about the Massie and Fortescue cases. She read through the newspaper reports, then googled the two famous trials.

Thalia Massie, a young white woman, alleged she was raped by five native men, although strong evidence contradicted her account. The trial of the five men ended in a mistrial because the jury could not reach a verdict. Angered, Thalia's mother, Grace Fortescue, a socialite related to Alexander Graham Bell and the Roosevelts, decided to take justice into her own hands. She had her son-in-law, Lieutenant Tommie Massie, recruit two Navy men to kidnap one of the acquitted men and beat a confession out of him. Failing to do that, they kidnapped another man, Joseph Kahahawai, the man in the photo. This time, the kidnap ended in shooting and killing the victim. He deserved what he got, Mrs. Fortescue told reporters.

The American newspapers called it an "honor slaying." In the last case of his career, even Clarence Darrow couldn't save Fortescue and the other defendants. The jury found them guilty of manslaughter. The governor, under pressure from the Navy and the US government, commuted the mandatory ten-year sentence to one hour served in his office. Four days later, Thalia Massie, her husband, and her mother boarded the steamship *Malolo* and departed to San Francisco.

Halia's grandfather Angel was living in Honolulu at the time. Everyone thought the tension in the city would ignite a race war. Her tutu Hani had lived through it all, too, but never once mentioned the incident. Yet here she had all these clippings and a photo of Kahahawai. She turned the yellowed pages of the notebook carefully. It had many more blank pages than written ones, and several torn pages. The written pages contained baking recipes, to-do lists, doodles, quilt drawings, bits of popular song lyrics. She recognized the lyrics from the Hawaiian Wedding Song: *Here I am waiting, Where's my beloved.*

Halia was about to toss the notebook on the throwaway pile, when she hit on a longer entry dated January 10, 1932.

> *Today, so many people went to pay respect at your funeral. So many people there wasn't no room inside the church. People say it was almost as many people as Queen Lili'uokalani's. Neighbors, friends, family, strangers, haoles too, went to say goodbye. I wanted to get closer to you, but it was too crowded. From where I stood, I saw a crucifix on your chest and a 'ilima lei. Even lying in the casket, you looked handsome in your suit.*

There were so many flowers everywhere it smelled like spring in the chapel. Before they took you to Our Lady of Peace, a man got up and started weeping and wailing that the haoles murdered you like they did his brother. Someone said he knew you. Your friends had some time to say goodbye, then your father spoke a few words. Policemen in motorcycles led a long line of cars to the cathedral. A beautiful ceremony. Thousands of people walked behind you to Puea Cemetery. I saw Mr. Sabatier there. He smiled and waved. I felt bad because I didn't wave back or even smile. I couldn't stand to see them put you in the ground. When they started singing, I ran back home, crying all the way in the rain.

They killed you. The haoles who tried to send you away for something you didn't do. Joe, you were my lei lehua. My waiting is over now. Since a little girl, I loved you. You were kind to me even when other kids made fun of me because of my eye. People were scared of you because you were strong. But you only used your fists in the ring or to protect people, even animals, like that poor dog that drunk was kicking. You came to her rescue and knocked him out. You didn't look for no trouble though it found you sometimes. Because you ran around with them boys from Kauluwela. You all liked to carouse and drink and got into trouble. But none of them really bad guys, though they made fun of me until you told them to stop. Deep in my heart, I knew you were a good guy. Every time you came into the bakery my heart jumped. You used to get bread for your mom, sometimes sweet bread, on special occasions a pineapple upside down cake. I always made sure to give you a little extra of the Kulolo, your favorite. You were sweet to me when you dropped in. Asked about my parents and we talked about people we knew from high school. When you left you always had a sweet smile. I kept waiting till the next time you came around. Praying one day you'd ask me out. I will never know what it's like for your lips to touch mine. For you to touch me. My dreams of us to-

*gether by the beach, kissing under the moonlight, will forever
be dreams. You probably weren't going to like a girl like me
anyways. A plain looking girl with a lazy eye.*

*I will miss your aloha every time you came to the bakery.
No more times will I see you walking to the market or down
School Street or in Kam Field. My heart is broken into pieces and my hope gone. Papa yelled at me because I said no
when Mr. Sabatier proposed. Mama, too. You ain't getting
any younger, they tell me. He's nice and all, talks to me a long
time in the bakery. But he's an older guy just looking for a
wife. And he's not you, Joe. You're gone. What am I gonna do,
now? Why they kill you, Joe? Why?*

She nursed her last glass of wine, still awake at dawn.

Kurata and Chang found their boss in underwear and T-shirt, facing the massive wall window in the bedroom. It was nighttime and
he had called and demanded they get their asses over to his house.
Neo Murdoch could be a pleasant man, but he had not built a
multinational company and amassed great wealth being nice. His
underlings read the edge in his urgent call. In a matter of minutes,
they had left the management compound where they lived and
drove over to his mansion.

The two men looked at each other. Kurata leaned in toward his boss.
Sir?

Murdoch raised his hand, still facing the window, head down now.
Listen, he said.

The two subordinates did, and they heard the chirping of the
coquis, which became clearer and louder as they concentrated.

Murdoch turned around. With his hair tousled, his beard looking scragglier than usual, and his eyes smaller than ever, he stared
at them.

What the hell is that? I'm jetlagged from my trip and can't sleep
with that racket out there.

Those are frogs, sir. Little frogs, Chang explained.

For little frogs, they sure make a lot of noise.

They seem to be a problem around the islands.

Well, I don't give a damn about that. How do we get rid of them?

The state is dealing with the problem.

So, they're here cleaning it up?

No, they're working in other areas, as I understand it.

That's not gonna help us, now will it, Kurata?

No, sir.

Set up a meeting with whoever is dealing with this problem. People come to a resort island for peace and tranquility, for God's sakes. Not to be kept up at night listening to this crap. Now, go. Make it happen. He waved them away.

Murdoch turned on his tablet and pushed down his earphones. He closed his eyes and listened to the sounds of a rushing river.

They were waiting for Neo Murdoch to make his entrance. Halia received a call at dawn to be ready and fly out from Maui to Murdoch's island on his private jet. No explanation other than it was urgent, and when she saw the others on the plane, she knew it was so. Now, around the large conference table, she spotted officials from the capital. Higher-ups from HISC and HDOA. Officials from Maui county. Business and tourism, also. And for the icing on the cake, Congresswoman Tessa Golub. To have all these individuals come to this billionaire's private island at his expense, something important was going down.

On the plane, her thoughts lingered on her grandmother. She tried to square the letter with the woman she had known as tutu Hani. A quiet woman, seemingly content to live in her husband's shadow. Everyone figured her eye made her self-conscious and shy, the reason why she rarely looked at anyone directly. They all thought her quiet demeanor was a generational thing. To Halia, she was a loving grandmother who taught her how to sew quilts, who prepared herbal remedies for all sorts of ailments. Occasionally, she spat out a few Hawaiian words that she and Alana thought were curse words. Now, Halia saw it all as a way to fold back into herself and a past she was unwilling to forget. Poor Hani. She wiped away tears and didn't know why she was crying. It just felt sad. All of it. The letter. The way Joe Kahahawai died. Her grandmother's unrequited love and yearning. The marriage to 'buelo Angel, now revealed to her. Or maybe Halia understood being with someone but feeling a desperate loneliness.

The doors opened and Murdoch marched in like an emperor. Kurata and Chang followed, leading a cadre of subordinates. He wore jeans, sneakers, and an expensive blazer. Amid the silence, he paced back and forth, with a slight strut. Turning to the assembled group, he leaned in, fists on table.

I've pumped hundreds of millions of dollars into this island. All along we've pursued a sustainable, green-friendly eco-tourism plan. We've invested millions in a desalination plant alone. I love the natural beauty of this island. That's why I bought it. So others can share it. As you well know, Paradise Development's efforts have cranked up the economy in this area. That economy is centered on folks visiting this little paradise. They come here to escape and relax. They want to forget their troubles and enjoy themselves. At night, after a day of horseback riding, surfing, suntanning at the beach, or any of the hundreds of activities that they pay handsomely to enjoy, they want to get some sleep and be ready for the next day. And, *this* is what's waiting for them.

He extended his arm and pressed a remote.

The noise of coquis chirping streamed out of enormous embedded speakers and filled every inch of the conference room. It was deafening and annoying. Murdoch turned it off and tossed the remote on the table.

I don't know who's in charge of exterminating these noisy little pests. Personally, I don't appreciate having to kill any living creature. Hell, we helped the community build the cat sanctuary to control the feral cat population on this island. But the state has allowed this situation to get out of hand. I hear they're invasive and don't belong in these islands. They're killing other native species. Now, they're threatening a billion-dollar investment. So ... I don't care how you do it. Get rid of them.

He gave them one last stare and nod and walked out with most of his entourage. Kurata and Chang remained with the head of the legal division.

Chang clearing his throat broke the silence. I think Mr. Murdoch has made his wishes clear, he said. How can we assist you with your plan of action?

Two days after that meeting, Halia found herself in Murdoch's island again, supervising an operation that felt more military than anything else. Congresswoman Golub had suggested that plane spraying the citric acid and water mix would be more efficient and faster. Every night for two weeks, the planes swooped down and strafed the flora. During the day, two hundred contracted workers walked with backpack sprayers soaking bushes and plants or sprayed from five cannon trucks. By the second week's end, crews were vacuuming the dead frogs into disposable bags.

Meantime, in Maui minimal spraying had occurred as resources were diverted to what Golub called Operation Tiny Kermit. Halia dreaded having to confront a situation that probably had worsened there in the two weeks she was on this small island resort. Murdoch's invitation to a dinner for the workers and supervisors didn't make her feel any better. Nor his congratulations for a job well done. Dressed in jodhpurs and boots, he toasted to evicting the little unwelcome foreigners for life. The dining area erupted with laughter and cheers. Halia got up and went for a walk. Outside, the night air was fragrant with plumeria and hibiscus. It was also eerily quiet, except for the murmuring of crickets and katydids.

Back on Maui, the war on the coquis continued. As she toured the battleground, the entire operation seemed like a perpetual impasse. They just couldn't get in front of the frogs' reproduction cycle. Hawaiians wanted the coquis silenced, forever, but no one wanted widespread aerial spraying. Or hordes of weekend warriors armed with powerful spray guns patrolling across the islands.

The absurdity of it all hit her when they asked her to present iPods and Xboxes to the area schools with the most coqui kills. Her refusal upset her supervisor, who had to do it. You know, she told him, I went into the life sciences, not mortuary sciences. That's real funny, he said, then hung up. It wasn't meant to be funny. Lately, she questioned how her career path had taken this turn. She loved biology because how things lived within ecosystems fascinated her. Working at her parents' nursery since childhood naturally developed her curiosity for science and led her to study botany. Now, at the end of her career, she was rewarding young people for killing an organism trying to survive.

On the first weekend back, she drove to her parents' home and lost herself again amid the stacked boxes in her parents' garage. She had finished reading Hani's letter and the newspaper clippings on the morning she received the call about the Murdoch meeting. Now, in front of her lay items from her grandfather Angel's life.

A framed photo of his son, Uncle Gabriel in uniform, probably taken before he went off to fight and die in the Pacific during World War II.

Memorabilia from her grandfather's own army days. Two round disks stamped with his name, rank, regiment, and nationality. Two postcards from Camp Dodge, Iowa, where 'buelo Angel was stationed, addressed to his first wife, Lucinda Morales.

The first card, postmarked August 5, 1918, had an illustration of a young woman sitting at a vanity table, reading a postcard. By her side was a photo of a soldier. Surrounding a pennant with Camp Dodge on it, the message read:

> *If you look in the mirror, somebody there you'll see, whom a soldier's boy at Camp Dodge is missing awfully.*

Halia smiled, shaking her head. So unlike her stern grandfather, she thought. He didn't write anything on that one. But on the second, postmarked September 9, 1918, in elegant cursive, he wrote:

Querida, sorry not to write sooner. Busy marching, training. First time shooting rifle. Big place here. Have everything we need. I'm okay. Hope all is well back home.
Kiss Gabriel for me, Angel.

Then, there was a letter dated October 16, 1918.

Querida Lucy

Sorry not to write back sooner. Been very sick. Me and lotta guys got Spanish flu. Spent much time in hospital. They separated us sick, white and colored, in the hospital like in the barracks. Some did not make it. Young guys training for war and dying from disease. Crazy. Tell you the truth, I thought I was not gonna make it. I kept thinking of you and Gabrielito and worry if something happened to me. The fever gave me bad dreams. My clothing and sheets got wet from sweating. I got stronger and they let me go from the hospital. They say we go fight in a month. Couldn't sleep much. Started thinking about the rain falling on the tin roof back in PR when I was a kid. Such beautiful music. The coquis, too. Their song on a rainy night used to make me sleepy. Ko-kee. Ko-kee. These memories help me forget and find peace. And I can sleep. Pray for me Lucy. For God to look over me and let me come back to you and our son. Our family together again. You both are in my thoughts every day. I miss you very much. Give our son a big kiss and hug for me. Tell him papi loves him very much.

Your loving husband,
Angel

The last letter, postmarked November 26, 1918, was short:

Querida Lucy,
The war is over. This Thanksgiving we have much to be thank-

ful for. I wish I could celebrate with you and Gabriel. I am so
happy my prayers were answered. They are going to discharge
us in a couple months. Can't wait to see you and Gabriel.
Until then I remain your loving husband, Angel.

From the family grapevine, Halia knew that both Lucy and their daughter, Cristina, died in childbirth. Her grandfather Angel had told her once that many years of hard work and sadness followed. He lived alone in a small apartment in Honolulu, working long hours at the pineapple cannery. Since he didn't have anyone to take care of Gabriel, he had to send the five-year-old to live with his grandparents in Maui. He met tutu Hani when he first went into the Kalani bakery for sweet bread. She was shy and embarrassed about her eye, he said, but if you could get her to smile, it was like the sun breaking through a cloudy day.

Angel kept visiting the bakery, sometimes just to see her. He bought so much bread that he had to give some away to neighbors. He knew she was a good person and would make a good wife, but when he asked her to marry him, she declined. When he saved enough money, Angel decided to move back to Maui to be with his son. His parents owned a plant nursery he could help them run. He told Hani he was leaving for Maui and wanted to take her there as his wife. This time, she accepted.

Halia soaked in the hot tub. She had emptied every box, sorted it all out. All that remained was to call the liquidator. As she relaxed in the bubbling water, she kept thinking how her people had traveled different paths to suffer similar pain. They struggled to keep the business going over a century. They committed muscle and sweat, their hands, to grow and nurture flowers and plants. Her mother loved growing orchids, tending to them with so much tenderness and attention that it made Alana and her jealous. Hani used to say our flowers help people remember. Halia remembered the disappointment on her father's face when she told him she didn't want to continue with it. How easy for the roots that ground you to shrivel, she thought. To lose their grip on the past. Easy to take for granted your family's sacrifices. Because you don't know them, or you pushed them back in memory. It doesn't take much, really.

She reached for the phone.

Alana, she said, I changed my mind.

The Coqui Whisperer arrived in the evening. He wore a head lamp and carried a plastic tube with a bottle at the end. He was a quiet, little man with a wispy mustache. They had found the plants and flowers infested with frogs. The person hired to keep an eye on the nursery after her mother died had not been doing a great job. Halia blamed herself for sending him checks without touching base. The man watered and misted the plants but never mentioned anything about frogs. He wasn't around to hear them in the evenings or at night. Neither was he checking on the plants themselves during the day, or else he would have spotted them. Or maybe he did but kept quiet to keep the checks coming.

After they decided to keep the business, the sisters drove to the nursery to check on things. When they arrived one evening, the noise was enough for them to know there was a problem. The Coqui Whisperer didn't hurt the frogs. His method was to imitate the male call and wait until the female came out; then, he would trap her in the tube and take her to a sanctuary.

The Coqui Whisperer took a few steps toward the nursery. He heard the frogs and pivoted around.

Are you kidding me, he said. I only do a few. You have an invasion here.

The sisters watched him take his tube and leave, and then looked at each other.

You know what you gotta do, Alana said.

Halia nodded. She didn't want to kill the poor frogs, but no one was going to buy anything. She had retired from her job, sold her parents' house, and invested the money back into the business. Alana's portion too, since she had agreed to help run the business.

I'll make the calls, Alana. But please, be here when they do it. I just can't.

The day Lou and the crew came to do her the favor, she decided to use the comp Murdoch gave to everyone for vanquishing the coquis. She went to the island and took a room. She sat poolside, sipping a tropical drink, enjoying her day at the luxurious island resort. Later, she took a walk. In the quiet sunset, she opened the aerated jar and released the pair. Walking away, she smiled as the male's call drifted into the wild.

CLEMENTE BURNING

THEY HAD TOLD HIM not to go. His oldest son had nightmares about it. Days before, his wife started crying and ran to the bedroom when that popular song came on the radio, the one about the plane crashing on Good Friday. His good friend José informed him the old plane they chartered had a history of mechanical problems, that the crew wasn't very competent. The plane had way too much cargo. He knew all that. It didn't sit well with him either. You know that weird, sad feeling you get when something just doesn't feel right? As he boarded that plane, he sensed it. He turned and knew his wife had spotted the sadness on his face.

Now, though, after it was all over, he has grown accustomed to being stuck between somewhere and nowhere. Eerily, he's adjusted well to this limbo state, as if he had experienced it before. At first, the sensation of living in a cage without bars rattled him. If he started walking, his legs would move but get him nowhere. All around the blankness changed color depending on his moods, as if these imaginary walls were amorphous huge screens. His mind was the projector and his emotions wrote the scripts.

Where he is now or what happened doesn't matter. Only a few things are certain. For sure, his life had ended too soon. He had had many plans. There had been so much to do. The undeniable truth is that his wife and sons had known he loved them. He hoped that would be enough to let him rest. His body had taken a beating. Playing eighteen years of baseball, the way he had, would wreck any human body. There wasn't a muscle or bone that hadn't ached that last season. So, he surrendered to the much-needed rest.

But Clemente knows the sense of rest is an illusion. Only the longing for it is real. He has always been restless. He suffered a lifetime of insomnia. There were nights when he couldn't sleep thinking about the next game or haunted by visions of early death. Here, where there is no desire for sleep, and death was a waiting game, a different uneasiness settles in.

He never experiences hunger or any desire, for that matter. There is nothing to do but think. So much time to contemplate, ruminate, analyze, deliberate, meditate, muse, reflect, ponder. Why? It is harrowing and draining, and was starting to feel pointless, hellish in a classical Greek kind of way. All he had besides these stormy thoughts—and the uneasy mind to generate them—were gossamer memories he lovingly nurtured and caressed as a wretched, lonely person would a faithful dog or cat. He waits for something to happen—what, he doesn't know.

His memories. The last one, vivid: the crystalline, turquoise water as it rushed into the plane. An oddly refreshing, warm salt bath cleansing his body. His agitated mind captured his wife and the boys before he glimpsed, through the window, the bright light filtering through the ocean. His body sank with part of the DC-7 into the Caribbean Sea, lost forever.

Clemente believes it's everyone's duty to help people in need, so how would it have looked if he had stepped down? Rumors about corrupt officials in Nicaragua diverting the aid concerned him. But he couldn't back down. No regrets. How could he regret anything? Even in the darkest moments, he counted his blessings.

And there were dark moments. The day his brother Luis died on New Year's Eve. That accident driving to visit him at the hospital; an accident that riddled his body with aches forever. Or his sister, Anairis, burning to death, which left a void in the family's heart forever.

He had received a letter once. I'm going to shoot you in the second inning, someone wrote, while you're playing right field in Three Rivers Stadium. Clemente imagined flying in the air, snow-coning a hard-hit line drive, and then hearing the shot. Falling to the ground, the pain slicing into his side, but holding on to the ball. His wife's face distorted with fear. Her hands covering her boys' eyes. The day of the game, he kissed his crucifix and said a little prayer before heading out to the outfield, but he never turned around once, not even in the second inning. He hit 2 for 4 with a home run to right field.

Other hate mail arrived and calls streamed from the stands. Written threats, insults in mocking Spanish accents, monkey sounds, tossed beer cans or other garbage. Comments from teammates and players. Not what Jackie suffered or endured, but enough to test his patience. Just like Jackie, during spring training in Florida, he ate meals in the homes of black families because hotels didn't serve black players.

Unlike Jackie, he got it from all sides. "Why don't you back up your black brothers," the black players would say. He wasn't black enough for some black fans. But some whites and blacks called him "just a Spanish-speaking nigger." Both made fun of his English, his accent. One time he remarked to a reporter he felt treated like a "double nigger." Stuck between two places and not belonging in either one.

Playing in the minor leagues, in Montreal, he used to eat alone. After a game, he'd walked in the old part of the city because it reminded him of San Juan, with its narrow, cobblestone streets and historic buildings. For a moment, during the summer days, he'd transport back home if he closed his eyes. Then a drunk would say "go back to Africa," or a passerby stared at him as he strolled around an alley. One time he and a younger white woman were chatting at a bar. An older woman stopped and stared at them.

Disgusting, she said, shaking her head and walking away.

He had to be honest. Even after the championships, and the awards, he never felt he belonged. Other Puerto Ricans didn't understand. He would tell them: I learned about racism when I came to the United States.

Clemente turns to something stirring in a growing light.

Un momentito, Momen.

A tall black man emerges out of the void.

Who the hell are you? No one calls me Momen but family.

The man strokes his stylish, bushy mustache, his big round eyes widening with amusement. An elegant suit dated him, but Clemente didn't know from when. His curly hair is parted neatly on the left side of a beautifully shaped oval head. He struts toward Clemente upright, with confidence.

Just another Afro-Puerto Rican, he says, but this one isn't all over the history books. He stops and stares. Unlike you, with all those books slavishly holding you up as a Golden God.

Maybe if you'd done something, you'd be in the history books.

The stranger smiles. Don't like your tone, brother. That was one of your problems, wasn't it? They said you were arrogant, a little temperamental. A bit of a big mouth.

The man slides his hands into his pockets and rotates to view their surroundings turn bright red. Look at you, the man says, getting all worked up as I speak. Here, have a seat.

Where did that table and chairs come from?

Just sit down and roll with it. Here, tomate ese cafecito.

Clemente stares at the coffee cup and saucer suddenly in front of him.

There's no coffee in it.

Of course not. No need to eat or drink anything here.

Then why offer?

Because even here—in this world of nothingness, manners count. Use your imagination, hombre.

Clemente sips the coffee, and it tastes familiar, like the coffee whose smell filled his nostrils early in the mornings before his mother woke him up. How wonderful to taste that black sweetness. Especially those days when he worked in the cane fields along his father, loading up bundles of sugarcane to the trucks. He closes his eyes, savoring the beverage, and he wants to cry.

The man smiles, a wide, inviting grin. Good, huh?

Clemente nods. Some pastelillos would go great with this, he says.

Don't push it, replies the stranger.

So, who are you, really?

Arturo Alfonso Schomburg, a la orden, he says, extending his hand.

Schomburg doesn't sound Puerto Rican, Clemente says, shaking his hand.

Neither does Walker. Schomburg winks and sips his coffee.

Clemente smiles, nods his head, amused. That was his mother's last name. How do you know so much about me?

Roberto, who doesn't know about you? Schomburg sits back on his seat and looks at him. A man with an inner fire that hit like a well-calibrated machine. A fire that made you run the bases like a burning madman. But that same fire—lord, you upset so many people.

It's a free country, he responds, shrugging his broad shoulders.

That's what I love about you. Schomburg leans toward Clemente. You really don't know you're a Negro, do you?

What a stupid thing to say—of course, look at me. I admitted I was black.

Admitted? Like it's some secret. Yeah, sure—You'd say you were black but in your mind that word had an asterisk after it.

Nonsense.

Oh, right. You learned racism in the United States. Really?

What's your point?

My point is you're still seeing yourself through the eyes of white people.

What the hell does that mean?

You want to know who I am? There's a library up in Harlem named after me. It contains the finest collection of materials on African and African diaspora history, art, and culture in the world.

I spent my life gathering and curating it. Most Puerto Ricans don't even know I existed. Don't even know I was born in Santurce.

Okay, so you want an apology?

Schomburg closes his eyes, exhales, the air bursting through pursed lips. He shakes his head and stands up from the table.

You know, a teacher once told me black people had no history. That we had not contributed anything to history. That we had no great historical figures. His words stung me, and I swore I'd prove him wrong. And I did. Every Puerto Rican must undergo that journey—including you. Above all, *you*.

With those words, Schomburg disappears.

Clemente spins around. He turns several times, but Schomburg is definitely gone. The man's sudden disappearance disappoints him, saddens him. Alone again, he is about to lie down on the cumulus-like layer of blankness shading into blue, when he remembers Schomburg's coffee, the table and chair. He recalls the comfortable, king-sized bed at home in Carolina. The one with the special mattress for his back. It materializes in front of him. He laughs, claps his hands, and throws himself on it. Around him everything turns golden yellow.

He mulls over Schomburg's words. He was rude and presumptuous. But the longer he contemplates the scholar's words, the deeper his mind wanders into the past. Pieces of memory drift into open consciousness, and then rush before his closed, fluttering eyelids. One memory jolts him up from his prostrate position. He stands and drifts into its sounds, sights, smells, all senses flooding him.

He conjures two faces. His father's downcast eyes, tight lips, rigid jaw. Across from him, Don Pepito, the big-bellied boss of the Victoria Sugar Company, his face blotched, a grin that belies his anger and frustration, the day he heard him chew out his father.

Clemente, Clemente, he had bellowed. The yields are low. Before his father could respond, the fat man with a waxed mustache went into a tirade about how everyone's job is on the line. Get me some strong arms out here. Why aren't you getting more moyetos?

he asked. His father didn't answer, which just angered the boss even more.

Coño, hombre, that's one reason why I made you foremen—so you could recruit more of your people. You got the back for this type of work and you don't get sunburnt so easy. That's the great contribution of negros to our country. He said this with gravitas and propriety as he wiped his face with a handkerchief.

I want more moyetos out here, cutting this cane. We need to increase production. Clemente was stacking cane far enough from the swinging machetes that he saw and heard the two men. He didn't like Don Pepito talking to his father that way. Why doesn't he talk back or tell him to lower his voice? The men his father supervised were working, but they were also listening to the exchange.

When they rode back home on the company truck, he asked his father why he didn't hire more "moyetos." Tensed, Melchor Clemente told his son, Don't use that word, Momen. It's not a good word. After a few minutes, with a smile, his father added, Don Pepito must see thousands of negritos in his dreams or under his bed. There aren't enough to work.

He understood what his father meant. In school, other children looked indio or trigueño, but no one could deny his ebony complexion. Once Miguel Santos screamed that he had bemba lips. He wanted to punch his mouth and turn his lips into bembas, but his parents would have been upset with him. They preached against fighting and getting into trouble in school. We work hard, his mother used to say. We don't need problems from your teachers. At home, he stared at the mirror to check his lips and came to the conclusion that they weren't that big after all. He had pelo grifo, nappy hair, but at least everyone said he's un negrito perfilao. A black boy with a nicely shaped nose and lips.

Is negrito a good word?

Of course. I call you negrito all the time, right?

And you call mami, negrita.

That's right.

They passed acres of rolling cane as they bounced down the dusty road back home. Clemente's young muscles ached from lifting cane bundles, but it's a good pain. When the truck leaves them walking distance from their modest house, Melchor turned to his son.

You know, Momen. It's sad to say, but sometimes black people are just not dependable. Don Pepito thinks he knows black people.

Why don't you explain that to Don Pepito?

He laughed and shook his head.

You want me to lose my job?

Everything washes out in a flash of blinding light and Clemente is standing in a hallway of his elementary school, the day the girl giggled when he gave her a caramel. Then, when she thought he wasn't looking, threw it in the garbage with a twisted face, shaking her hand like it had germs. The light's energy propelled him to a corner of his high school, where Amalia, the pretty brown girl with big hazel eyes, who smelled like gardenias, told him she couldn't date him anymore because he was too dark. At a park, his friend Tomás stopped playing with him, and later wouldn't look at him as he walked with his father, whose nostrils flared as if smelling something bad every time he saw Clemente.

The powerful light surges and flushes through him, images cascading past. The fear and subdued disgust on the priest's face as he offered him the host during mass. The surprised looks of light-skinned classmates when he contributed something in class, glances never reserved for the light-skinned team captain. He became overwhelmed with the idea that his truest white friends, if they ever transcended their sense of superiority over him, always pitied him for being darker. He had buried those moments, those ideas, somewhere cavernous and arcane. The power of his confidence had kept them there.

His entire childhood is opening, ripe for review. Perhaps here were the reasons why he gravitated to baseball. For why he stayed in his room tossing a scruffy baseball against the wall until nightfall. Why he spent hours alone, hitting bottle caps with a thin broomstick, hiding in an imaginary world of baseball where crowds chanted his name. A place that blocked everything bad and ugly. A place far from buried memories that hurt.

The spring Clemente headed to Montreal to begin his professional baseball career, his family gathered to bid him farewell. His mother cried and kissed him. His siblings hugged him hard, teary-eyed. For such a close family, to have one of their own leave to such a far, foreign place was sad bordering on tragic.

Clemente was about to get into his brother Matino's car to depart for the airport, when his father appeared with a fawn-colored fedora. He offered it as a going-away gift. This will keep your head warm up there, he said. Clemente thanked his father and at his insistence put it on and then got in the car. He took it off and set it on his lap right after his brother sped off.

Does he really expect me to wear this? he asked his brother, raising the fedora from his lap.

Come on, Momen. He gave it to you with love, Matino teased him.

It's an old person's hat.

Not true. Papi says all the men up north are wearing them.

All white men, you mean.

His brother said nothing and noticed Clemente's mocking smile turn into a smirk. They rode in silence. After the car reached the highway to the airport, miles from home, Clemente lowered the window and flung the hat toward the passing grasslands. He sat quiet the rest of the ride.

The Pirates were aboard a train bound for St. Louis to play a three-game set after dropping a game to the Cubs. They were in the middle of a brutal twelve-game road trip which wasn't going well and will end worse. It was mid-May in Clemente's debut season and they were struggling at the bottom of the league, now chugging along on train traveling through America's heartland.

Halfway into the trip, some teammates napped, a few played cards or read newspapers. Others escaped to the lounge car for drinks. Clemente couldn't sleep. He had never traveled to this part of the United States and absorbed the passing view out of the window. Distant farm houses, bigger than those on the island. The occasional tractor rumbling along. Trucks toppling with rolls of hay. The stink of pig and chicken shit in the air. Acres of wheat fields blanketing the landscape for miles. They reminded him of the cane fields back home.

An erratic drumming broke his daydreaming. He turned around to the back and Pres, the back-up first baseman, was striking a bongo with sausage fingers. No rhythm whatsoever, Clemente thought. The playing was bad enough, but he began wailing, grunting, and making monkey noises.

The Pirates only had one African American player, Curt Roberts. He slouched in his seat, disturbed from his slumber by Pres's antics. He looked back once and turned around to gaze out the window with a quick sneer. The three black Latino players, Clemente and the Cubans Lino Donoso and Roman Mejias, shared bothered looks but ignored him. The other Latino on the team, Felipe Montemayor, shook his head and smiled, amused. Felipe was a light-skinned Mexican.

Pres bought the bongos in Havana, on one of his trips to Cuba for a taste of the night life.

Damn, I love Cuba, he said several times. Love me them cigars, the rum, the weather. Especially the señoritas, he said with a raspy growl, tapping on the drums.

Today, he was in rare form, banging with a passion never before seen, inspired to show off his repertoire of grunts before he let loose with a string of pseudo-Spanish verses.

Lino Donoso had had enough. He was sitting across from Clemente, by the aisle, next to the manager, Fred Haney, who had the window seat. He had remained quiet through Pres's antics, but mocking his native language put him over the edge. Clemente heard him whisper, hijo de puta, as he was about to stand up. Haney gripped his shoulder. He stared at the pitcher, eyes flaring, his thin lips tighter than usual. Sit, he ordered.

The manager straightened his short body and turned around toward the back. Pres kept serenading his teammates, eyes closed now, slapping the bongos with impiety.

Hey, Pres, could you put the drum away. You givin' me a headache.

Come on, Fred. Just having a little fun. Pres taps the bongos, grinning.

Haney swaggered to the back, the train speeding through a tunnel. He stopped two rows short and leaned in.

Put those fuckin' bongos away, or I will shove them so far up your ass they'll be callin' you bug-eyes for the rest of your miserable career. Then I'll fine you a hundred.

The lanky first baseman slipped the bongos under his seat and crossed his arms. Haney plopped back into his seat, huffing, red-faced. Baseball wasn't as much fun anymore. He understood that coloreds had to break in. It was the right thing to do, but he hated all this other shit that it had brought. Donoso turned to his manager and whispered, thank you. Haney nodded and closed his heavy eyelids to sleep.

At Union Station in St. Louis, the traveling secretary, Bob Rice, gave each of the Latino players and Curt Roberts their spending money in an envelope.

Your hotel reservations are at the Midtown Hotel.

Donoso and Mejias exchanged looks. The white players were boarding cabs to head to their hotel.

Why we don't go with them, Mejias asked.

The hotel they're staying at doesn't allow coloreds, Rice explained. Sorry, fellas, not much we can do.

Clemente couldn't speak English well, but having it taught in Puerto Rican schools under American law, he knew enough to translate.

Que mierda, Mejias said. Then, in the best English he could muster: Montemayor can go?

Rice turned around and saw the Mexican outfielder walking with the others.

He's white, Rice responded, confused.

He's Latin American like us, Mejias said.

Roberts laughed. Rice threw up his hands, turned around and walked away, his head down.

Welcome to America, Roberts said, walking toward a cab. Come on, amigos, we can share the ride. The hotel's not far from here.

Clemente stared, mouth open, watching the last cab full of white teammates drive away. No one in Puerto Rico had ever refused him entrance into any place. His family was poor and couldn't afford to stay at a fancy hotel. But someday, he would walk into the Caribe Hilton, Normandie, or Condado Beach Hotel without a problem. He told this to the others in the cab, and Donoso laughed.

In Cuba, even Batista couldn't get into the Biltmore Yacht Club, referring to the country's dictator. They told him he was too black and he was a mulatto.

Mejias didn't laugh. I thought here it would be different, he said.

Mejias didn't come from Havana, like Donoso, who understood Cuban racism firsthand, having been born and raised in the capital. He experienced racism there from white elites who were decidedly better off than the black population. Like Mejias, this was his first year in the States and for some reason, he also believed it would be better.

Roberts sat in the front seat of the cab, listening to his teammates talk heatedly in Spanish, and shook his head. He didn't understand what they were saying but knew what they were upset about.

Y'all gotta understand you in America now. White man don't give a rat's ass if you speak another language. You black, you black. Negro, he says, pronouncing it in Spanish, as he rubbed the side of his cheek with two fingers.

Donoso nodded. He's right, he said, after Clemente gave a quick translation.

Best to lay low, Roberts added. Just deal with the shit, is all I'm saying. That's what Jackie told me and I'm sticking to it.

Everyone in the cab, even the cab driver, was black. But to Clemente, they were culturally different. A part of him felt insulted by Roberts's comments. It was as if the African American totally dismissed that the other three were from Caribbean countries. That their first language was Spanish, and their history and experience as black men was different.

I'm not black like you, Clemente said.

Roberts smirked and laughed. The cab driver looked at the rearview mirror and snickered.

Okay, rookie, Roberts said, tell that to the white man.

They drove the few blocks to the Mill Creek Valley neighborhood where the hotel was located. The row houses were rundown, and everyone was black. Their hotel wasn't elegant. It was old and in another lifetime it probably had been something else.

At least here we're not going to get the evil eye, Donoso said. To which Mejias responded, Amen.

They checked in and Roberts told them he was going to take a nap.

I'll meet y'all downstairs at the Peacock Alley Lounge for dinner, if you up to it.

The Latinos nodded and left for their rooms.

Que mierda, Mejias said, as he grabbed his suitcase and headed for the elevator.

Roberts was already downstairs having a drink and listening to the live music. He had shaved and appeared refreshed. The three Latinos greeted him and sat down to order drinks before their meal. Donoso and Mejias each had a beer. Clemente didn't drink so he sipped water. The quartet playing featured a handsome young man singing a sad tune. He also played trumpet, melancholy and sweet.

Clemente couldn't make out all the lyrics, but it wasn't necessary. Sitting there in that lounge, listening to the singer's tenor voice and his moody solos, his heartbreak was not about a lost love, but it hurt just the same.

Roberts noticed Clemente's expression. He remembered back to last year when he sat in this lounge, a rookie and all alone. The only black player in the team. Now, he wondered if it was all worth it.

Sad, ain't it? he said to Clemente.

The rookie nodded and smiled.

Chico, I'd rather be dancing to some mambo, Donoso said.

Or listening to Celia and La Sonora, Mejias added.

The Latinos laughed, and Clemente explained Afro-Cuban music to Roberts, how it's livelier, all about dancing and having a good time.

Roberts nodded and smiled. Y'all lucky this ain't the blues, more to himself, because he knew they wouldn't understand.

After they paid for dinner and the quartet took a break, they went their separate ways. Restless, Roberts invited the others out for some livelier music. The Latino players decided to play a few hands of Brisca in Donoso's room. They didn't know the city or area, which inhibited venturing out. That and their limited English.

Roberts turned to Clemente.

Listen, I know we different, but deep down we're dealing with the same shit. Stick together, brother. This is a hard country for black folk, and it's gonna be baptism by fire for you. He patted him on the arm and left.

On the train back east, Clemente couldn't sleep, although they had been traveling for hours. The setting sun's coral rays slanting across endless golden fields soon made him drowsy. It was night when the train slowed down somewhere in southern Illinois. He peered out the window. About two hundred yards away a fire raged. He and some of his teammates gathered around a window for a better view.

Standing next to Clemente, Roberts turned and bent toward him.

Bet you don't see that in Porto Rico.

The cross mounted on an island of whiteness burned; the smoke fingered upward to the black sky.

Suddenly, the fire's burning glow expands, totally encompassing Clemente. When it fades, he finds himself back within his familiar blank surroundings. Yes, the segregated hotel, the cross burning that night. Roberts explained its meaning, but he forgot about it next day. It's an American thing, una cosa de gringos, and he had a game to play. But why repeat it? Why are these memories haunting me? he wonders.

Out of the mist, Schomburg reappears, holding two empty cups of coffee. He offers Clemente one. It smells good. Schomburg smiles as Clemente takes it.

Momen, let's talk, he says.

They sit down at the table and a vibrant sky blue surrounds them.

GO MAKE SOME FIRE

EVERY DAY AFTER CLASS with his tutor, Antonio peddled to a secret spot, where the waves would cradle him to sleep. Eyes closed, he inhaled the humid air; and leaning into the light, the sea embraced his body. Daydreaming, he soared with the breeze into the sky. But today, a nagging reminder snapped him out of his afternoon reverie.

Jumping on his beat-up Humber, he cycled down the dirt road, past fields of sugarcane. In less than ten minutes, he swung into Esperanza Street and arrived home. He patted dust off his clothing, swatted sand and beach grass out of his hair. Taking a deep breath, he entered and faced three solemn individuals, seated in the tiny living room sipping coffee. He caught his father's creased brow. The stranger, an older gentleman, appeared bemused. With a flushed face, his mother shook her head and whispered at him to wash up for lunch.

After washing, and the introduction to Mr. Bisbal, his father's supervisor, they sat down to eat. Both men worked for Snow White Sugar after the war and the American occupation three years earlier. While they ate, Bisbal explained how the American

Commissioner of Education was sending Puerto Rican boys and girls to school in the United States. Juan Serrallés, their boss, promised to find eligible students among the workers' children. He informed Antonio's parents that their son had been selected.

Mr. Islas was happy to hear the news. He hired a tutor for Antonio because he could not afford the only private school in Ponce, and there were no public schools. He wanted an education for Antonio; wanted him to take a position in the company. As Bisbal spoke about the wonders of this American school, Mrs. Islas looked at her only child with equal parts of fear and frustration.

After lunch, they all escorted Bisbal to the door to say goodbye. With the door closed, Mrs. Islas spun around and slapped her son. Never, ever, embarrass us like that again, she yelled, following him into his room. You're seventeen years old, not a child, Antonio.

His father entered the room. She turned to him, arms crossed, her face twisted in an angry and worried frown. How's he going to survive in America, Luis, if he's always somewhere with his head in the clouds? Her husband nodded and waved her away. Antonio slumped in the corner of his bed, sobbing. His father sighed and patted his son's knee. In a voice as calm as Good Friday, he told him everything would be wonderful in the American school.

You always wanted to travel. Think of all the new things you'll see. The people you'll meet. It's an adventure.

As he looked at Antonio, bent and tears dripping off his nose, he thought how lonely they would be without their only child.

In spring, Antonio Islas boarded the SS *Philadelphia* along with forty-two other young Puerto Ricans en route to New York City. For five days, he shared stinking toilets and slept on an uncomfortable stacked bunk bed in a crowded, noisy compartment holding hundreds of passengers. The daily ration of slop flung into his tin pail made him miss his mother's cooking.

In New York harbor, a man named Joshua Baylor came to claim them. He marched them through lower Manhattan. Even the ones from San Juan couldn't believe the stench, the noise and the number of people herding past alleys, where rats the size of small dogs feasted on stacked garbage. Antonio gaped at the tenements and pasty faces jutting out of windows. He covered his nose and mouth as they passed mounds of horse dung, and then a dead horse rotting by the curbside. They slogged through streets and sidewalks crammed with carts full of produce and goods, skirting horse-drawn buggies and the rare chugging automobile, until they reached the ferry to the Jersey City terminal.

On the train, Antonio struck up a conversation with classmates José Osuna and Santiago Montaño across from the girls. Elusive at first, Osuna warmed up and even smiled. Castula Rodríguez was the opposite. Sitting in the back of the car, she had her friends laughing. Montaño looked at you with a quizzical face that either expressed lack of intelligence or fear. Antonio understood the fear. He was thousands of miles from home and only spoke a few words of English. He didn't know where they were going and what to expect.

At the Carlisle station, they staggered out of the train. From another car, Antonio saw dozens of children spilling out onto the station.

Move along. Don't pay them any mind, Baylor said. They're orphans, not Carlisle students.

The orphans looked frightened and lost. Antonio wondered where they were going. He thought of his parents and what they were doing, and if they missed him yet. After collecting their belongings, the students marched the one mile to the school.

Baylor prodded them on until they reached the high archway entrance to the Carlisle Industrial Indian School, the name in bright red letters. Underneath it, in elegant Latin script, Antonio made out the words, *Indum Necate, Hominem Salvete*. As the Puerto Ricans walked past the gateway, they saw brown faces peering behind bars from an isolated building. Later, he learned those students had violated the rule against talking in their tribal language.

They stopped in the middle of a large open field. In formation they waited, thirsty, hungry, clothes streaked with perspiration, their bodies aching. The spring sun was dimming; the crisp wind giving them their first Pennsylvania chill. To his left, Antonio saw a gray-haired man dressed in cavalry regalia, mounted on a horse, riding toward them. His sword rattled; the feathers on his helmet flapped in the wind. He reminded Antonio of Don Quixote. The man turned the brown Morgan toward them and stopped. With small sunken eyes that flanked a large protruding nose, he inspected each one in line. He looked like a man whose thin lips had never broken into a smile or laughter.

I'm Lieutenant Colonel Richard Henry Pratt, the superintendent of this school, your new home, the Carlisle Indian Industrial School.

He talked in a growling voice, weary for having spoken similar words countless times. Most of them couldn't understand a word. Even Osuna, the most proficient in the language, blinked in confusion with every word. So, they missed the warnings, the rules and regulations, the spirited coda with advice to lose old ways and progress to a brighter civilized future. Then he galloped off, to where, no one knew.

The bell would ring from the tower outside at six o'clock in the morning, followed by reveille. After changing into his gray, military uniform, Antonio marched with the others to the dining area. They ate in silence, their backs upright against chairs. All of them shoved food into their mouths, staring forward past each other. The staff walked around to maintain silence, shushing anyone who whispered or as much as giggled. His family talked a lot during meals; most of it his father, but they had a conversation. This silent eating bothered him, more than the blandness of the food.

The only decorations in the dining hall were banners celebrating past sports and musical achievements. He stared at los indios. He had never seen Indians and wondered if they would be naked and wearing feathers in their long hair. But their hair was cut like theirs, and there were no feathers anywhere. A girl stuck out her tongue and made him turn his blushed face.

A whistle alerted them to their work detail. For Antonio, this meant the carpentry workshop, where he learned to make and fix furniture for the school. Castula got placed in the kitchen, which she hated. They sent Osuna to the fields to learn how to farm. After work, they marched to class. When they had precious minutes to chat, in rushed whispers, Osuna complained to him about the classes. Arts and crafts, and music, he found frivolous. The English class disappointed him. It wasn't teaching him anything new, although it allowed him to practice. Antonio agreed. Like the others, he had thought they would be preparing for professions.

After lunch, they worked and studied until the recall bell summoned them outside for the ceremonial flag salute. Colonel Pratt led the salute in uniform on foot, the sun reflecting off his polished boots.

In bed, Antonio wondered how he could continue this routine for years. He remembered how his father talked about his clerical job at the factory. It was so boring he often drifted to other thoughts, like snow, cowboys, the depth of oceans, watching a movie, or kissing a girl. He couldn't understand how his father loved working at such a tedious job. Or why he needed to travel thousands of miles to be in a place just like Snow White Sugar.

One night, he was tired but could not sleep. Outside, a screech owl's repeated trembling song caught his attention. Slipping out of bed, he walked cautiously to the window, a few feet from his bed. A full moon lit up the frame and glistened through the windowpanes. The owl continued its sad trill, but he couldn't find it anywhere on the trees. Disappointed, he headed back to bed, but on the way noticed a miniature drum by the side of a student's bed. Antonio bent down for a better look.

It was a beautiful drum made of brown leather, the sides painted in alternate red and blue triangles. The head had an image of an eagle done in the same colors but with a bright, yellow background. Kneeling on the floor, he picked it up along with the drumstick.

His tutor once brought a drum to one of his tutorials. They had been studying the Taino Indians, and he claimed the drum was an authentic one. That wooden drum was elongated and had holes in it. He wanted to play the drum, but the tutor told him it was too fragile to withstand any drumming.

The owl's tremolo was so rhythmic and persistent that Antonio had to resist the temptation to accompany it on the drum. As he lay down the drum and the stick, a pair of wide black eyes trapped his. Antonio stumbled backward and fell. Someone stirred outside and walked toward the door. The Indian boy shoved the drum and stick under his bed. Antonio tip-toed quickly back under the covers. Baylor opened the door and glared into the long, dark room. Seconds later, he closed the door. Antonio released his breath and heard the boy's muffled laughter.

By summertime all the Puerto Ricans were unhappy with the school. They whispered their complaints about everything. Castula, who wanted to be a teacher, joked that all she would be able to teach was how to make grits and mashed potatoes. Osuna mentioned he had written and complained to his parents, and Antonio was stunned to hear others did the same. He understood their concerns, their regimented days were harsh, the work brutal, and what they learned would help minimally in the professions they yearned to have. But he was happy to be away from his parents, even though he missed them. He found the lessons more acceptable than his tutor's ranting and harping. The food was foul, but after hard work and a day full of activities, it satisfied his hunger, and he had gained weight. His letters to his parents never complained.

He had also made a new friend. The day after the drum incident, he noticed one of the boys grinning at him. The owner of the drum, Antonio Tapia. Tapia was a Pueblo from Santa Fe, New Mexico, and he spoke Spanish besides his native Tewa. When they realized they could communicate in this shared language, they conversed in Spanish as if speaking in code. They whispered during classes and at night from their beds. Tapia introduced them to other Pueblo Indians, and he grew to like these new friends. They were generous and kind, and sometimes it felt as if he were talking to Puerto Ricans.

During the summer, Carlisle arranged students to work in nearby farms as domestic servants or farmhands. Colonel Pratt told them that the outing program allowed them to stay in homes of good white people so they could learn the benefits of civilization. The students not working in farms ended up in factories or in the ironworks. They were happy to earn wages for their labor but did not know the school took a percentage.

In late June, the school dispatched several of the Puerto Ricans to the Arnwald onion farm. Typically, students from the same tribe never went as a group on the farming details, but Pratt had convinced Arnwald that Puerto Ricans were adept at agriculture. Sitting in a hay wagon on the way to the farm, Osuna and some of the other Puerto Ricans joked about Antonio's Indian friends.

Soon, he'll start wearing feathers, Osuna said.

Why don't you dance and make some rain; it's damn hot, added Montaño, which made everybody laugh. Antonio stared at them as they shook from laughter, mocking him, and it struck him how much they all looked like Indians. The brown skin, the eyes, cheekbones, nose—everything. Or was it that Indians, with their cut hair and Western clothing, now looked like them?

Why do you make fun of them—they could be family, he told them.

Osuna's nostrils flared. I'm no indio. We're not like them. We have people looking out for us. He looked around, then leaned in. My parents contacted Luis Muñoz Rivera, he whispered. And he's visiting the school to check on our complaints.

The others sprang up. Really? asked Montaño. Osuna's confirmation made them all excited, even Antonio.

Muñoz Rivera was an exiled political leader living in New York City. While in the United States, he published a newspaper. When he received news of the bad treatment of the Puerto Rican children at the Carlisle school, he wrote to Pratt requesting a visit in August and was granted one. This bit of news made the trip to the onion farm more tolerable, and for that moment they felt a sense of solidarity.

Once they started the farm work, Antonio swore the Puerto Rican politician could not come fast enough. Arnwald worked them for fifteen hours, giving them ten-minute breaks for water, and half an hour for lunch, which they ate out in the fields. Like the others, he had no experience farming and did not have the foresight to wear a hat. Stooped, he dug up the bulbs from the ground and tossed them in a bushel basket. When full, another worker took the basket and replaced it with another one. At the end of the day, after a meal of onion soup and bread, he huddled into a small shack with bunk beds. There he slept, unbathed, his stomach rumbling until the morning bell called them back to work. Antonio would hate onions for the rest of his life.

In the second week, their work started slipping. Osuna attempted to lift their spirits, but the others, particularly Montaño, would not have any of it. The hell with these onions and these yanquis, too, he said, turning the basket over and sitting down. His lips were parched, and rivulets of perspiration rolled down his forehead. From the corner of his eye, Antonio saw Arnwald strutting toward them, pulling something out from his side. He had no time to warn Montaño. The farmer pounced on the boy, striking him with the whip, the dozen leather strips slashing across his thin frame.

Get up you lazy bastard, get up, he yelled, with every lash, as Montaño cowered on the ground. Antonio jumped and covered Montaño.

Please stop, please, he cried, in English. He caught a few lashes before Arnwald ceased, breathing heavily, eyes bulging, and strapped the short whip back on his belt.

Good then. Tell this good for nothing tipi tom to work or he'll get more of the same. He looked around to the others. I'm not paying you to sit, he said. You're no better than a bunch of squaws.

Get up, he yelled at Montaño. He picked the boy up by the collar and tossed him back toward the onion field. They all resumed work and continued until the sunset bell.

They did not complain to anyone at school. Montaño made them promise. His father had asked several favors and even bribed someone to get him into Carlisle. He would be disappointed and angry at his son if he stirred up trouble. Antonio understood Montaño's predicament. Their families had pulled strings and spent savings to receive what everyone had assumed was a privilege. They remained quiet about the incident and resolved to make their families proud.

They withdrew, even more than the other Puerto Ricans, who also wished they had never left the island. When they heard about a runaway, their spirits lifted, but soon sank to learn the person had been caught. If someone escaped, whatever hope came to them about doing the same crashed with the anxiety of having nowhere to go, worrying about starving or getting lost. During bedtime, Antonio heard prayers and sobs in the darkness. He thought about his father shaving for work. The smell of coffee mixing with his after shave. His mother preparing eggs or maizena while singing. He missed his bicycle and wondered if his father kept it for him or gave it to one of his cousins. He recalled his secluded beach. The salty mist on his skin, the sea lapping at his feet, the sand between his toes. Then, he would close his eyes, tears forming at the corners, and fall asleep.

He found comfort in Tapia's friendship. Tapia was going to graduate in two weeks. Antonio had learned much from Tapia, not only about coping with the school, but also about Pueblo history and culture. Tapia talked about customs, traditions, legends, food; taught him a few words in Tewa. They became such close confidants that Antonio told him about the onion field. Tapia described students working in steel plants returning with burns on their arms and faces, others were maimed.

There's funny stuff going on, he whispered. A few girls, their bellies grew. We didn't see them for a while and when they returned, they didn't have bellies. I've seen strange women walking in hallways at night, and in the morning being taken away. We have seen bottles of moonshine in the basement.

He took a deep breath and exhaled. My heart and body ache from this place.

Antonio nodded and both stopped talking as their carpentry instructor approached to inspect the chair they were charged to repair.

On the day before graduation, Tapia shoved Antonio awake. He stood bedside, half his face bright with moonlight, dressed in day clothes and holding the drum and stick.

Come, he said. Stumbling with sleep, Antonio dressed and followed him toward the window at the end of the rectangular room. Together, they opened the heavy window and slipped outside into the full moon's luminescence. Tapia took off running, drum tucked under his arm, stick in hand, past the bandstand decorated with bunting for graduation. Antonio kept up, following into a stretch of spruce and pine trees and finally toward Letort Creek. Not knowing where they were going, he smiled as the air hit his face and his heartbeat quickened.

They stopped running, breathing hard, and laughing. After crossing a plank bridge, they hugged the side of the creek and walked until they settled on top of a large boulder overlooking the water. They lay there and stared at the moon that looked close enough to touch. Low water crept past scattered rocks and pebbles, forming tiny rapids, under the stream of moonlight. The constant noise of water against rock calmed him.

98   Tapia told Antonio to gather some dry twigs. Together they piled branches, twigs, and pine conifers within a circle of rocks. Tapia took two rocks from his pocket and within minutes started a fire. With firelight, Antonio saw green moss covering nearby rocks, the whiteness of the rapids below, the surrounding bushes, and, up above, the silhouetted canopy of giant oaks. As he looked around, he approved of his friend's secret hideout.

At one point, Tapia grabbed the drum and stick. Listen, he told Antonio. He drummed slowly, accentuating every beat so Antonio could follow. He handed the drum and stick to Antonio and gestured to play. With just minor corrections, Antonio played the sequence.
Continue, Tapia said, and stood up. He wiped the rock surface clean of debris. Then he spread his arms and hopped, head down, to the drumbeat. The young dancer chanted as he shuffled and hopped in a circle, flapping his arms above his head then bringing them down. He stopped and bent his knees and lifted himself on his toes. With mincing steps, he hopped to one side, then another, head down.

Faster, he told Antonio. He picked up the pace and Tapia circled faster, arms extended as far as they could, while he hopped on one foot at a time. His body soared and swooped and landed.

Antonio stopped drumming and stared with admiration.

Eagle Dance, Tapia said.

They sat by the creek until Tapia suggested they return. After putting out the fire, they walked back in the dark beauty of the forest, listening to the screech owl and the rustling creatures in the bushes. Nearing the school grounds, they passed the cemetery. Look, Tapia said, pointing to headstones with names of former Carlisle students who never made it to graduation or back home. Lined in six rows, they stretched thirty or so yards. Antonio walked between two rows, and as he drew closer to the headstones, he made out some names, and under those, their tribe. Many were marked Unknown.

They climbed through the low window, which they had left slightly open, changed their clothing, and slipped into bed. No sooner had his head hit the pillow, Tapia fell asleep. But as tired as he was, Antonio kept seeing Tapia dance, remembered the smoky smell of the campfire and how it glowed on Tapia's graceful body. That vision melded into a dream where he saw Tapia flying around rows of headstones extending up to a burning sky.

No one from Tapia's family attended the graduation. Many parents couldn't afford the long trip from the West, or Midwest, or in Tapia's case, New Mexico. Non-graduating students made up a good portion of the audience. It was a quick ceremony to everyone's relief. Dressed in military regalia, Pratt gave the same gruff speech to the graduating class he had given to the Puerto Ricans on their arrival. Awards were handed out; fifteen graduates received diplomas. The remaining students were allowed a few minutes to wish their friends and former classmates luck and say goodbye.

After he had packed the few items belonging to him, Tapia gave Antonio the drum and stick. On graduation day, he took out the two flint rocks and handed those to Antonio, too.

Go make some fire, he said, and hugged him.

During the summer, most of the Puerto Ricans could not afford the trip to the island. Osuna was one of the few and everyone thought he would not return. But he did. Those who stayed had to work to pay their room and board. Antonio worked gathering potatoes, peaches, and blueberries. On one occasion, as reward for his hard work, the school gave him the opportunity to stay with the Stantons, a childless couple, in their house outside of Harrisburg. There, Antonio learned to serve food and do odd jobs for Mr. Stanton until classes resumed.

With the new school year, a fresh group of students arrived. Among them three Pueblo Tesuque students who told Antonio that Tapia had been arrested and executed for shooting a soldier. In assembly, Pratt mentioned the incident. Red-faced, his veins bulging in his neck, the colonel called it a disappointment and a stain on the school's reputation.

This young man's decision to return to the blanket shows the
dire consequences of this terrible decision, he said. Use this opportunity we graciously give unto you to uplift yourself and your people. Move forward. Not backward.

Late that night, Antonio fidgeted in bed. He bent over the side of the bed and pulled the drum from underneath. He wanted to play. But instead he slipped it under the bed, along with the flint rocks. He had to urinate and headed to Mr. Baylor's office in the corridor to explain his need. Baylor slept, head tilted against his shoulder, snoring loud and ragged. Not wanting to disturb him, Antonio headed to the washroom and saw a light coming from Pratt's office.

He had never entered the colonel's office, which was a good thing, since mostly only students in trouble would. The colonel was rarely in his office late at night. Antonio peeked in and saw Pratt slumped against the long black leather backrest of a reading chair. At his side on a small table was a bottle of bourbon and a glass. The office was big, full of bookshelves and books, decorated in blue, heavy curtains over the windows; stolidly centered, stood an ornate mahogany desk, immaculately uncluttered.

What are you doing up, boy? he asked, his voice gruff and sleepy.

Toilet, Antonio said, pointing in its direction.

Pratt's eyes narrowed. Antonio had never come close to this man, who seemed like a mythical creature to students. Now, he saw the scarred face from childhood smallpox and the large nose. Eyes that with the liquor appeared more hidden than usual.

I know you were his friend, he said. Probably will end up just like him. He dismissed him with a flick of his heavy hand. Go and do your business. Go and return to the blanket for all I care. You ungrateful bastards. There are people who would rather kill the lot of you.

Antonio stood frozen at the threshold. Leave, the colonel yelled, and he ran to the washroom.

When Luis Muñoz Rivera arrived, the school lined up the Puerto Ricans to meet him. They were scrubbed and cleaned and wearing their best uniforms. Antonio swore they all had received bigger portions during lunch. After getting a tour of the facilities, Muñoz Rivera entered the meeting hall and greeted them. A man with slicked back hair, a bushy mustache covering his lips and wearing a suit too tight for his plump body, he stood holding his hat and asked questions about the school. He spoke in Spanish and leaned toward them to listen when they complained about the vocational rather than professional training. He smiled at the whining about the food, the long school day, and the work in the fields. No one said anything about Montaño's beating. Antonio didn't mention the odd occurrences Tapia had revealed to him. After shaking everyone's hand, including the school's staff members, he left.

Two weeks later, Osuna received a newspaper clipping of Muñoz Rivera's article. They passed it around, stunned to read he agreed the school was a good trade school and that their parents had probably deceived themselves to believe their children would become lawyers, doctors, and teachers.

That night Antonio slipped away to Tapia's rock, and after several minutes trying, managed to build a fire. There, he lay within the quiet, balmy air, staring at the stars. He missed his friend and wished he could have learned the Eagle Dance. As a screech owl's trill tore the night's silence, he tapped Tapia's drum, softly at first, then louder, until the banging became hypnotic and his fingers blistered.

The young Dakota Sioux boy was new and like the others resisted his hair being cut. He kicked and pulled back his head when Baylor held out the scissors. He bit the teacher's hand and burst into the open field. Other teachers ran after him, but he was fast and quickly disappeared into the forest. Pratt ordered a few of the men to track him down and bring him back. He won't get far, he said. Hours later, they found him drowned in the creek. Antonio teared up watching the boy's corpse carried back to the school.

He waited until there was a full moon and packed his meager belongings into a pillowcase. He slept on Tapia's rock and rose at daybreak to walk toward the road to Harrisburg. By late afternoon, he had arrived at the Stantons' house. Having worked for them during the summer, Antonio knew the Stantons as generous people, Quakers he trusted would not turn him back to Carlisle. In his best English, he told them he didn't want to stay at the school any longer. That he would work for them until he could leave for New York City and return to Puerto Rico. Antonio's desperate, teary face touched the elderly couple. They had heard rumors about Carlisle among the Friends at their meetings—that everything was not as rosy as Pratt painted it and agreed to help him.

Antonio lived and worked at the Stanton house through the winter. He was such a diligent worker that in the spring Mr. Stanton, a master printer at the *Telegraph*, hired him to clean the shop and arrange the typecast boxes and bottles of ink. He was a fast learner and soon grasped the basics of line casting. It was messy, dirty work, and often he walked the streets of Harrisburg with the indelible inked markings of a printer's devil. He enjoyed working at the shop, the camaraderie among the journeymen and other apprentices. But he yearned to hear Spanish spoken, to eat food now a memory, to see his parents. To revisit his hideout and taste the salty sea on his lips again.

When he had accumulated enough money for a train ticket to New York, he left. Osuna once mentioned if he were to run away, he would head to La Colonia, a Spanish-speaking enclave in New York. Arriving in the city, he asked people where he could find this mecca of his people, but he sooner found rows of cigar factories. He inquired about employment in several before he landed a job with Ottenberg and Brothers as a roller. The work was mechanical and tiring, but the factory hired a reader to read the workers the daily newspaper and literary works by authors like Zola, Hugo, and Dickens.

He rented an apartment on 28th Street, a few blocks from the factory, and after work strolled through the neighborhood around the new Flatiron Building, searching for places to eat or to browse in bookstores. The pace of the streets invigorated him. The noises made him feel alive. He grew accustomed to the rapid, harsh sounds of New York English, dodging the horse-drawn buggies and frantic pedestrians alike. He even welcomed the odorous pressed bodies packed in subway cars on his way to a roof garden for a stein of beer and entertainment. After a few beers, he sometimes ended on Soubrette Row for female companionship.

One Saturday after work, he meandered through crowded sidewalks in search of a good cup of coffee when he stumbled across a sign—Club Borinquen—spelled in chipped red letters above a storefront. His heart jumped to see the Taino name for Puerto Rico on such an unsightly sign. *Was this La Colonia?* Maybe people inside would help him return home. He shoved his hand into his coat pocket and rubbed Tapia's flint rock, which he carried wherever he went.

He hesitated at the doorway, questioning if he really wanted to return. He had written to his parents only once since leaving Carlisle, to inform them he had left and was now living in New York City. He didn't give them an address, knowing they would be disappointed and angry. Not only his parents made him pause. New York had transformed him into a man content with a carefree life, and Puerto Rico seemed so distant and long ago. Maybe, he thought, walking through the faintly painted door, he would change his mind.

What first struck him was the unmistakable smell of strong coffee, like the one his mother brewed, and then the smoky earthiness of tobacco. Cigars stacked on an opened humidor sat next to a cigar cutter shaped like a rooster. Every single man in the room turned from their cigars and cut through the gauzy smoke to stare at him.

A tall, stout, dark-skinned man, with large penetrating eyes, approached him.

Hello, brother, he said, in Spanish, extending his hand. I'm Alfonso Schomburg.

Antonio shook his hand and searched the faces across the room. They seemed familiar although strangers. In the back of the room, a large Puerto Rican flag hung on the wall. A framed map of the island underneath. The room contained memorabilia from various parts of the island: Wooden Santos; figurines of the three kings; miniature porcelain pieces of bulls and coquis; a machete enclosed in a glass case. Various instruments: guitar, cuatro, conga, guiro. African masks and face jugs, slave shackles, pottery. Paintings of famous Boricuas lined the walls, most of whom he did not recognize. A large bookcase contained books written by Latin American, Puerto Rican, and Spanish authors, along with French and English titles.

Can I help you? Schomburg asked.

Antonio turned toward him. Something past the man's shoulder caught his eye. A statue of an Indian against a wall. He had seen many of these in front of tobacco shops on his many walks through the city. This one wore a feathered headdress, a necklace of some animal's teeth hanging around his bronzed naked chest. By his thigh, he cradled a bundle of cigars with his left hand. Right hand on forehead, the Indian gazed into the horizon. Antonio squeezed the rock settled in his pocket.

Brother, are you lost?

RIP AND RECK INTO THAT GOOD LIGHT

for Julian

T.J.

I hit him once. Not one of those little nalgazos in the butt when he was a kid. I backhanded him when he cursed at me. I ain't having any of that. He respects me and his moms and anybody older than him. Period. Looking back, I should've slapped him a few more times. Koki, with all her psychobabble, thinks you can't spank a kid for nothing. She reads too many books written by people who don't live in the hood and think everyone sees the world with the same eyes. Try living in the South Bronx like we did and see how far those fancy ideas get you. They'll get your ass handed to you, that's what.

My life wasn't messed up because my parents slapped me once or twice. I had it coming, to be honest. I gave them trouble and made life hard for my moms, even after my dad split. Instead of helping her I made it worse. She slapped me, yeah, and she handled the Puerto Rican mother's WMD—la chancleta—like a ninja. That slipper would fly and wham, hit you in the head. Or she'd whack your ass with it like she was playing paddle ball. I never felt abused.

It's not like if you smack your kid once in a while it's abuse, you know. Unless, you have no idea how abusive it is to grow up in a neighborhood like ours.

These streets will eat you up if you weak. And they were even worse back when Koki and me walked them. Kids today fall apart for any silly thing. You best toughen up if you intend to survive. And now what? Are we supposed to ground him? That's a laugh. He's never out anywhere. Take away the phone? You kidding me? We can't afford phones for ourselves and we don't believe every teen needs a phone. You get food, a roof that don't leak over your head and clean clothes on your back and you thank your parents every day for your blessings. If you ground him, it's a chance to read the books he stacks in a corner or to listen to that crazy rap music. You take that away, he finds something else to do. Like that time Koki grounded him—no music, video games, or books—solitary confinement—for breaking curfew and he wrote lyrics for an entire album. This kid lives off being alone.

Meantime, the vice principal of the school, cat named Rosado, tells us Xavie's acting up. He and his posse of nerds, he calls them. Writing up school walls. How you know it's him, I asked. They're tagging lines from famous poems or rap lyrics, he answers, with a smart-ass look on his face.

Screw the theory; bougie ideas don't mean a damn thing out here. They're like prayers with no postage. Better make your kids toe the line before their attitude lands them in jail or gets them killed.

KOKI

I should have given him more time, more attention, more nurturing. What did I know about being a mother? I was sixteen, a child myself. Our little freak, that's what we called Xavie. He would do things everybody in the family found strange, like reading every line on a cereal box, or my dad's *Daily News* from cover to cover when he was only four. He started speaking in sentences before two. Drawing amazing pictures of faraway worlds when he was in second grade. He was always scribbling. He used to draw and write stories that he bound together, like books. We had no idea how truly intelligent he was. When they tested him in elementary school and told us he was gifted, we didn't know what that meant. T.J. was upset because he thought they were checking out his privates. The school wanted to skip him a grade. We said no because we thought other kids would make fun of him. There were no schools for gifted children near us so that was the best they could do. They were trying to challenge him, that's what the principal said, because he was bored and restless. For me, struggling day to day, I couldn't understand how more challenging life was supposed to be, and how that was supposed to be a good thing.

Only my mom, she knew from the start how smart Xavie was. Because she really raised him those early years. He's a genius, you just don't understand him, she would say to us, and we'd laugh. T.J. and me, stoned and buzzed from cheap beer at one of the club's hangouts. Stupid old woman, I used to think. She only went as far as third grade; everyone's a genius to her. A hick from the island, like my dad.

I couldn't stand them back then. Old school, strict. A girl's not supposed to be hanging out in the streets like a "macho," they'd tell me. I couldn't go out anywhere. My two brothers went everywhere and did anything they wanted. Then they moved out and left me with my parents who were waiting for me to marry so they could move out and return to the island. That was their plan. That and I had to take care of them hand over foot. It was like I was holding them back from their dream. When I hit sixteen, I said enough and started going out. I'd return late or sometimes the next morning and get slapped and hit. But I didn't care.

We were wild, all of us, searching for our own space, and the streets called us. We turned our backs on parents and found family with the clubs. That's what we called them, not gangs. Like they were an organization you joined for socializing rather than bop-ping. The Reapers controlled the territory around Crotona Park, where we lived. So that's who took me in. That's how I met T.J. At a club party in a dark basement.

Everybody respected T.J. He had cred. He studied martial arts and even boxed professionally for a while, until he found it more re-warding to beat up on rival gang members. Every girl wanted him. He had the charisma, the body, the cat-like green eyes. The poster child for a bad boy. Everything that's important to a teen girl, right? He hit on me something fierce, but I thought he was too conceited. He also had a temper, which I didn't like. The more I got to know him, the more I realized he was old school, gentleman like, even, with me at least. And his temper flared most when something was unfair or wrong. He was a fighter; always had your back. That's why the Reapers made him war counselor. I knew he was getting it on with other girls, but he didn't have anything serious going on with any of them.

I fell in love. It's that simple. Fell hard because he treated me with respect and after a while, I knew he loved me, too. Love as young love goes, anyway. Two young people desperate for atten-tion and a little TLC. It got to the point I hung out with club members just to see him. We started chilling together, sharing a joint and just talking. It was an escape from all the negativity sur-rounding me. By Christmas, a little after my sixteenth birthday, we were celebrating in Papo's crib, an apartment in an abandoned building. One of many the Reapers used to avoid police harass-ment. And boy did they harass us. They'd stop us walking in our own neighborhoods; take our denim gang jackets. Beat anyone who spoke back or had the nerve to look at them in the eyes. Sometimes they'd break into a club's main hangout and round up members.

So, we were always looking for a place to just chill without being harassed from family or cops. That Christmas Eve, Papo was staying with Margie, his girlfriend, and let us have his crib. We were already high from smoke and Colt 45. We danced slow jams, made out, and smoked some more. We had our own little Christmas party, and T.J. gave me a Christmas gift, a bracelet with heart and skull charms. I felt so bad because I didn't have anything for him. He told me all he wanted from me was to be his girl and I melted.

We made love for the first time on a musty mattress lying on a rotting wooden floor. I was a virgin and frightened but also excited. He was gentle and went slow, asking me if I was okay every step of the way. In the background, Bobby Caldwell was singing "What You Won't Do For Love" when T.J. whispered he loved me in my ear. I could have died right then and there. In a way, maybe I did.

T.J.

Koki's too hard on herself. We were both young and stupid back then. We messed up getting pregnant, but it happened, and the folks were not helpful at all. My moms went crazy. She told me flat out not to bring no baby into her house. That she wasn't about to raise no kids after failing with me—she said it just like that. Told me and Koki to get an abortion but she wouldn't pay for one 'cause it was against her principles. I get into a fight with her about her attitude and she throws me out of the house. Go be a big man with your little wife, last thing she tells me as she slams the door on my face.

Koki's parents were all bent out of shape, too. Her moms slapped her right in front of me, started pulling her by the hair, tossing her head this and that way. Had to twist her fingers out of her hair. Swear to God, if it wasn't her mother, I would've decked her ass. So much screaming, my god. For nothing, cause what's done is done. They told us we had to have it, gave all this religious mumbo-jumbo, so I say okay, let's do it. I'm in and I'm down to marry Koki, too. I moved into her parents' apartment, into Koki's room, which didn't go over big with her father. We should be married to share a bed, he said.

How stupid is that, right? He gave us crap all the time, but mostly directed at me. You ain't no man, he would tell me. A man takes care of his wife and kid. And on, and on.

One day I came back from the club stoned and wasted. But he jumped all over me just 'cause I grabbed something to eat from the fridge. Munchies, you know? I pay for that food and this roof over your lazy ass, he tells me. The way he said it just ticked me off. Fuck you, I said, and he comes at me. Now, I'm not going to let this old son of a bitch touch me. No way. So, bam! One punch to the face and he goes down. Doña Luisa starts yelling at me. Even Koki's screaming "why you hit him." They both trying to resuscitate the old geezer. I walked out and slept over at Papo's.

Things didn't get any better after Xavie was born. Koki and me got married which made her folks happy, but we were still living at *their* place, eating *their* food and bangin' in *their* bed. We kept living the gang life. Getting stoned, partying, and banging. Coming home late, high and sometimes scarred and bloodied. The old man would throw us some dirty looks, but pretty much kept to himself. The old lady calmed down a bit, too. All that mattered to her was Xavie. She loved the baby and taking care of him. Truth is we had no clue about being parents. Yeah, Koki changed Pampers once in a while, and fed him, but her moms pretty much raised Xavie. The Reapers owned us, and we were okay with that. But that was the past and I ain't got time to cry about it.

But all that was long time ago. Now, we got this situation with the kid. Besides vandalizing the school, he and his homies are roughing up other kids. Xavie's got my build, and he's even taller than me already. On top of being super smart, he's learning to push his body around. Never have liked bullies and my kid being one is something I'm not okay with. Rosado says Xavie's bored on account of being some kind of genius. He's got so much potential, he keeps saying with that sad, constipated-looking face. But I'm thinking my boy is not such a genius if he keeps doing stupid. And if he gets his old man really, really angry, he's maybe not using his intelligence much.

That whole conversation with Rosado was a big waste of time. Bad enough I had to take off from work, lose money, to listen to Koki and him sound like they're on some radio talk show discussing "feelings" and "inner self." Manny, my boss, is telling me, Dude, let your old lady take care of that. 'Cause I'm the shop supervisor and it's a busy month. He don't like anyone taking off for what he considers fluff. And on the other side I'm getting Koki giving me this guilt trip: He's your son, T.J. We *both* need to get involved.

Jesus. I'm between a rock and a hard place and it's all a no-win for me. So, I go and after spending an hour with this Rosado guy, we got nothing resolved. Basically, we were warned that disciplinary action will happen if Xavie continues. Tell me something I don't know. Suspension, expelling him, whatever. Meanwhile, he's listening to that hip-hop music driving all these kids loco. They all gangsta wannabes now. What a joke. They have zero clue what that's like. One thing, though. I know Xavie's acting up. But they're also blaming him for all kinds of stuff happening at that school. A window breaks, it's Xavie and his boys. Someone clogs the toilet with paper, that's the Islas' kid again. That's ain't right, and I'm not down with that.

KOKI

We were in a deep, dark place. Gang warfare was getting heavy. In the early days, if we'd fight, even the girls, we smeared on Vaseline and went at it with our fists, our bodies. It was always easy to get a knife or knucks but then everyone wanted a gun and they were easy to get. With guns and drugs, it got bloody. For the first time, I was scared. You don't understand death until you see someone you played Double Dutch with in the streets, who would come over to your house to eat and hangout—to see that person with a big hole in her head.

Or so jacked up you got to take someone's word it's your friend in that coffin. Fear and anger drive you to crazy things. I beat up people good back then. I'm ashamed to admit it; but it's easy to condemn unless you understood everything going down. We were not sociologists or psychologists studying youth gang violence and culture. We were living it. Kids, just kids, living in neglected working-class neighborhoods, trying to survive long enough to become grownups.

It didn't help that the media made it worse. I remember that photographer coming around, staging those fights, like the one with the knife. I saw it in the magazine and wondered how people could be so stupid not to notice us laughing in the photo. The few white folks who did thought we were laughing because we loved the violence, like we were savages, but we were laughing because the guys were going all ghetto for the camera, all for show. Those photos didn't give the whole story, which outsiders didn't want to hear anyway. They couldn't understand with all the problems this was our community, our people, our home. Most people were living normal lives on the little they had while a lost minority raged war against each other. Killed each other instead of battling those bringing the war on us. That story? Never got told.

I was one of those teen soldiers, and I felt like I was going through PTSD. I sunk deeper into darkness. T.J and me, we were each other's lifeline. We clung to each other to save ourselves from drowning. But we were really helping each other sink. The Reapers did not tolerate drugs. Many people think we were all druggies. In the beginning, because we modeled ourselves after the Lords and were down to help our communities, no hard drugs was one of our rules. We would drink a little and smoke reefer, but nothing like smack, cocaine, or the crack that came later. No stealing, either. We were supposed to have the community's back, their respect, and we couldn't achieve that being drug addicts and thieves. Not all the clubs followed that code. The Reapers did.

The only code I followed was the one that got me through the day, and that meant a little smoke and coke. When crack hit the scene, it was cheap, and the high put its claws on me. Got to the point where I couldn't hide it from anyone who wasn't blind. T.J. talked to the club leaders, but they were all military when it came to the rules, all hooah hooah. They lined up, gauntlet-like, and gave me my medicine. As I walked through that line they smacked, punched, and kicked me until I wasn't anything more than a raggedy doll thrown to a corner. Six guys had to restrain T.J. He kept screaming he was going to kill them all. Papo, his best friend since childhood, our son's godfather, stood in front of the biggest and baddest Reapers. We got no use for junkies in the club, he told T.J. Leave and take your crack bitch with you. They stripped off our denim colors. I was bleeding and bruised on the floor when they ripped it off me. T.J. just stared at Papo, speechless. He nodded and looked away, tears in his eyes. That's when I started crying. He picked me up from the floor and carried me out of that basement. All I kept saying was, Sorry, baby, I'm so sorry.

After that I knew things had to change. I got my GED and enrolled in Bronx Community. T.J. took a training in car mechanics and found a job at the garage. Everything was going fine, but it was still all about us. Mami was the one taking care of Xavie. She would look after him when T.J. and I were trying to get back on our feet. Then that day at the hospital. When papi called after I returned from classes, I flipped. He couldn't tell me what was wrong, so I jumped on the bus and went to St. Barnabas Hospital. Mami was asleep on a chair next to Xavie. I walked up to him and grabbed his little fingers. He was hooked up to an IV and that's when I lost it. I started sobbing and woke mami up. Carmen, she told me, no llores, m'hija, no llores, and then she came over and hugged me, which only made me cry more. T.J. came a few minutes later and the doctor told us Xavie had a stomach virus and was a little dehydrated but would be fine. Your mother saved his life by bringing him in when she did, she said.

To see your child in bed like that brings it all home. From that moment on, T.J. and I swore to focus on Xavie. We moved into a nice apartment on the Concourse. We were both working, making decent money, and happy. We believed we were finally a real family.

XAVIE

Taft High? I'd describe it like a jungle, but that'd be an insult to ecosystems everywhere. At least a jungle's organized for a purpose—here, it's just chaos. When you go through those metal detectors anything can go down. Niggas selling squares or even some yayo. Shorties blowin' trees in hallways. Gotta wait till someone finishes getting head to use the stall, and they don't even have the decency to wipe skeet off the toilet seat. The worst minds of my generation wasted by too much Mortal Kombat, dragging their drawers through corridors, talking back to punk-ass teachers 'cause they can. At the end of the day, no one's learned a damn thing, so what's the purpose 'cept to warehouse us, keep our asses in seats and pour BS into our heads. I'm tired of being locked up to learn.

Sometimes I disappear up to the school roof. Yesterday, when Mrs. Burger sat reading the newspaper and everyone was taking a test I finished in ten minutes, I slipped up there. Nobody noticed; they never do. I read and dropped some lines in my notebook. Looked out to the city: Concrete, burned buildings, and empty lots of garbage. *A heap of broken images, where the sun beats.* I think: Why you so hard, New York? I love you, but you ain't breaking me. No. *I won't take your handful of dust.*

I went back to class and wrote on my test: Nas be right: an incarcerated mind dies.

The teachers, they mostly don't give a damn. Clock in; clock out. They think we all losers; they only here for their check. That's all. They talk to us like we're morons; like we been deprived. Screw them all. Only Mr. Levin awright. He cares. His old man is this rich dude, head of HBO, but he's down with us. He goes the extra mile. He's okay with us rappin' in class, breaking down rhymes as part of the curriculum. And his literary chops are keen, man. He's feeding us Shakespeare. Boom! The Romantics, the Lost Poets. Bam!

The others, they a joke. It's stupid easy, dude. I been blown out of my mind before taking their tests and aced them. Sometimes I wonder how these mofos even get certified, you know? I mean, they follow the book to the tee, and then if I quote something from somewhere else, that I know is right, they tell me stick to the book. The worst one is Mr. Klavan. Oh my god. That is one racist, flag-waving, chauvinistic asshole right there. I argue with him all the time. Moms tells me to chill it with him, but I can't cause he's spewing that nasty, ethnocentric garbage he calls history, but it's *his*-story, you know what I mean? And my homies, they need to hear *our* story.

The dukes be ragging on my ass for what's going down in school. They gangbangers gone straight who think the entire world changed with them. They're in this little rose-colored, white-picket-fence, you-can-be-whatever-you-wanna-be, American Dream bubble that I'm always bursting. Pop! There I go again, making it real for the parental units. Man, the scene out here is no better than when they were my age. It's probably worse cause it creeps up on ya. Taft is wack. The teachers—except for a few like Mr. Levin—are mental thieves who should be sued for intellectual malpractice, and only fools believe things be getting better. Wu-Tang talked about you best protect ya neck, and they out in Staten Island. That's like the ghetto minor leagues.

So, I stay alert, keep my eyes on the prize, cause the prophet Tupac was right: there is death around every corner, holmes. Me against the world, you know what I'm saying? I'm gettin' mine when I can—bring on the cream. School's a waste of time. My daddy and momma's dreams won't see the light of tomorrow's darkness, so Ima gonna rip and reck into that good light. They say I'm smart and treat me stupid. Say the world's my oyster but trap me in a brick box. It's too ironic for rhymes, bro. Too tragic even for Shakespeare.

T.J.

Rosado called and told us we had to talk. This time he wanted to meet on a Saturday morning at the Cosmos Diner, which Koki and I found strange. When we got there, he was sitting at a corner booth at the end of the diner. He had to tell us something he couldn't tell us on school property.

Right now, I'm not the VP of Taft High. I'm a friend worried about your son.

Just tell us, I said.

He leaned toward us and whispered, I found this in his locker. He slipped me a Ziploc bag of weed under the table. I'm supposed to report this, but I can't. I just can't. I want to give you a heads up before it gets worse.

He had this painful look on his face, and I couldn't look back at him. I was ashamed. Pissed. But I was also liking this guy. He's right on. As we're having our coffee and breakfast, he pulls up his sleeve and shows the tat of a skull with crazy red eyes wearing a German-style helmet. The Savage Skulls logo. We all looked at each other, laughed and shook our heads, because our gangs had nasty fights back in the day. We called ourselves mortal enemies.

Right before he left, he said, You know Xavie's potential. And I know you know how this can play out. Please. Save your son. He picked up the tab and split. Koki and I sat there for maybe another ten minutes, drinking coffee and looking out the window in silence, until her sniffling began.

When I got home, I headed straight to Xavie's room. Wait till he wakes up, Koki said. But, I'm like, No, let's deal with this now. These kids act like they invented every single trick in the book. I dragged him out of bed, and he started bitching about his privacy. I overturned the mattress and found a big bag of weed and another of pills. Searched the closet and in an Air Jordan box found six hundred dollars, mostly in twenties. And a Glock.

Son of a bitch, I keep yelling, walking around the room like a wild man. Koki told me to calm down but that made me angrier.

He was on the floor, sitting against a wall, half asleep, half bored. I picked him up by the collar and stood him up.

What's this? I asked, shoving the bags of weed and pills in front of his face.

You know what it is, he answered, real smart-ass.

Why you doing this, Xavie? Koki pipes in.

, The name's X, he said.

Don't bullshit us, Xavie. Why you selling this garbage at school?

He wouldn't answer. He stood there and smirked, like we're lame idiots. I grabbed him by the throat. You think this is funny, you little prick?

Let him go, Koki said, so I pushed him back, hard, and he bounced off the closet door.

Xavie, this is serious. They're going to expel you from school, arrest you if you continue.

My wife, the voice of reason, right? The kid looked at his mother and said, At least I'm not a crackhead like you were.

I once saw Koki stomp a girl unconscious, after she had dug her nails into her face, and punched her to the ground. The demon that possessed her then came back. She jumped at Xavie and started slapping him, threw him down to the floor and I had to peel her off him. She was breathing hard and crying. You little shit, she said, and ran out of the room.

My son was staring at me like we're about to fight to the finish. I shook my head and started toward the door.

Yeah, best get out of my room, old man.

I turned around, took the Glock from under my belt and tee. Pinned him against the wall, one forearm against his neck, the gun pressed hard on his forehead.

Is this what you want, huh? 'Cause this is how's it gonna go down for you.

He didn't know I emptied the magazine. But he stood there, eyes locked on mine.

Go ahead, press the trigger, nigga. It's always the good ones gotta die.

I looked into his eyes. The same ones I used to look at when he was a baby. Back then they'd be all over my face, and he would smile once he knew it was daddy. Now, I couldn't find anything there, not even anger. He was looking through me to some place I could never see, wouldn't want to see. I backed away.

Koki was in bed, crying. I sat by her, squeezed her shoulder, stroked her back. Just when we were about to call it a night, Xavie turned on the stereo and started playing his music loud.

XAVIE

My parents exiled me to paradise. Paradise, that's what they think. That was the big idea for saving me. Send the kid down to Puerto Rico. Instant redemption for everyone. 'Cause in their minds, everything's awright with the island. What can be wrong where there's palm trees, sunshine, and jibaros. 'Cept palm trees drop coconuts on your head, dude. This brutal tropical sun will turn your skin into cancer bait, and the jibaros are rude hicks who don't give two carajos for Nuyoricans like me. Nah, man, this is no paradise. Ain't no gangsta paradise, that's for sure. A pastoral nightmare is what it is. The flip side of the American Dream. And that's what the dukes done sentenced me to.

Yeah, I was slinging. Making serious money, too, till the old man flipped out. Nasty scene with moms. Didn't mean it the way she took it. But it's the truth. Better to sell than use. I mean it's too pragmatic for the parental units to grasp. Dude, I was only dealing weed, X, and bennies, no big deal. Stacking Benjamins for college. Loan out some to friends. Like Tito, whose moms got sick and had no money for the doctor's visit. And Lettie, for the abortion. Other times for stupid shit like treating them to the arcades. You don't know the times I wanted to buy my parents a little something. Get moms a CD player for her salsa tunes. Pops, a new pair of work shoes to replace the raggedy ones he wears.

But they went crazy on me. Now I'm stuck in this island prison, sentenced to heavy mental labor trying to figure out these island Ricans. It ain't easy, let me tell you. The colonized mind is a desert with no oasis, bro.

The folks think it's better here? That's a joke. The school I go to is even worse than Taft High. I can pass the tests blindfolded. Can probably teach the class. I correct the English teacher all the time. They're doing math I was doing two grades ago. It's sad. You should see the school—right out of *Little House on the Prairie*, I swear. Sure feels like the frontier out here.

I'm in the middle of nowhere, in an island going nowhere stuck in the middle of nowhere. Sucks big time. Las Marias. That's the name of the town. Who were the Marias? Who cares? This is my grandparents' hometown, so the official caregivers send me down here. The abuelos decided to move to this cesspool 'cause the Bronx was a jungle. Now, they're like in a *real* jungle. The irony never ends with these Ricans, I swear.

I love abuela. I'd give my left arm and kidney for her, I would. If I make it big rappin' gonna buy her a big house on the biggest mountain in PR. I help her out around the house, too. Go to the supermarket with her, cut the gargantuan weeds around the house. Rub her feet when she watches TV. Anything she wants, she got it. But, man, this is a sorry-ass, mountaintop solitary, one road-get-me-the-hell-out-of-here, shoot-me-now-before-I-die-of-boredom town. I'd say it's godforsaken but that would require a Supreme Being caring about this place enough to know it exists and to then say fuck it. Maybe, that's the idea: lobotomize my frontal lobe with boredom. Numb me into submission.

Whatever. A playa's gotta play, bro. I spend my tropical days and nights just chilling with a few other Nuyorican kids who are into rap like me. The exiled like me with no home to call our own but a song to sing. The abuelos too tired to bother. They've been sucked into that vortex of stupidity called the idiot box. So, me and my crew hang, we blow a little, break down our lines to the waves on the beach or from the cordillera to the wind. We try to meet some señoritas, dance a little, stare at the stars like we're in a romantic flick. We pass the time hitching rides. We see a nice ride we like, and we hitch it. Who knew they be Ricans with enough cream to buy a Lexus or a BMW? We nationalize it in the name of the Nuyorican National Army. Ride around till we tire of it, then torch that shit. Dump it over a hill. Let it rock 'n' roll, trailing smoke and fire all the way down. It's a beautiful thing to watch.

You think I'm some type of monster? Judge me all you want, 'cause I don't give a fuck. World gave up on me a long time ago. Why should I stress over what it thinks of me? You don't hurt my hurt. You don't live my shit. From where I stand, the world's fucked up beyond repair. Why should I think it cares?

KOKI

They had him at the morgue in Mayaguez. T.J. and I flew into San Juan on a rainy weekend. Had to rent a car and drive hours to the west coast. Papi called to give us the news. It was hard to understand him because Mami was crying hysterically in the background. They asked us to identify the body. When they unzipped the bag, it took us a minute. His body was bruised. His face swollen and partly burned. I looked for scars and beauty marks; those that weren't burned. I spotted the one shaped like a kidney bean by his left hip. It was our Xavie.

We already knew. I felt it, anyway. Even when we decided to send him down to PR. He was a gift we didn't deserve. That we never should have gotten. He was better off with my mother. The island was safe, and it would settle him down. That's what we thought. When they told us he stole the car, it was the first time we heard. Mami would tell me he liked to party and hang out with his friend, but she didn't know anything about the cars. He never wanted to talk to us over the phone. He told us the day we put him on the plane we were dead to him. Every rebellious kid says things like that growing up. He'll mature and one day thank us, I thought. But I couldn't help feeling, coming home from the airport, that I might never see him again.

We flew his body back home. Because we didn't have a plot, we decided to cremate him. One of his friends suggested a little ceremony in Crotona Park. That's what we did. Invited family and friends to scatter some of his ashes near the park's amphitheater, where he once performed. Some of his friends rapped in his honor. Other people came up and said sweet things about him. How he was a loyal friend. How he would give you his last dollar, the shirt off his back. T.J. whispered, He was better to friends than his own parents.

T.J. wants to try again. Have another child. We're young, he says. But I feel old, like I've dried up inside, every part of me. I don't think I have another kid in me. Maybe God doesn't want to give me another chance. T.J.'s too dumb to notice I haven't been using anything for years. Something is wrong, but maybe it's really right.

It's been only a few weeks since we said goodbye to Xavie. I look at photos when he was a baby, a toddler, his crazy teen years. And I really can't *see* him. It's like he was always a mirage.

I used to look at him and think he wasn't really our son. They switched him at birth, I used to tell T.J. Somewhere, there's some dumb kid living with parents—doctors or lawyers, scientists—who are wondering what went wrong.

And we killed their kid.

GRANNIES GONE WILD

OH, I'M SURE SHE'S seen it. She can't be one of the few on the planet who hasn't. I just know it. 'Cause she's always on social media. And she's not the type to call right away if she did. She's sitting somewhere in that big house of hers, with a Mai Tai and vaping up a storm. Angry and embarrassed at me like always. I'm sure she doesn't want to talk to me, less look at me. Disgusted at me right now, I bet. Well, let me just say I'm freaking disgusted, too. At myself! For driving myself crazy thinking about this stuff. All I've done since I returned from Cancun is worry about what my daughter's going to think and say to me when she sees that crap on YouTube.

I had a great time with Dolores and Maddie. A vacation of a lifetime. One that I've needed and deserved for a long time, and all I pictured was her in front of her tablet, mouth wide open, thinking there she goes again. The more I think about it, about that scrunched-up look on her face like she's about to puke—you know what? The hell with this. Screw her attitude. Screw her judgment of me and my life. I'm not going to wait for her to come around to call and lecture me again. 'Cause that's the only time she calls me anyhow. When she wants to sound off and bring the old lady down.

I'm tired of her anger and disappointment. I don't care anymore. I'm not the perfect mom. Okay, I get it. I wasn't like the moms in that chuchi college upstate she attended after I busted my ass working to put a roof over her head and food on the table. That isn't important to her because it wasn't a house in the suburbs or organic food, right? I am so tired and done with her—and this. I just kept thinking about it, and it kept pissing me off knowing what was coming down from her. And it made me realize I don't need her negativity in my life. She doesn't care about me. She won't even let me see Addie as much as I want to. Probably thinks I'm gonna give my only grandchild brain damage or something. So, that's why I want to set the record straight about what happened.

First, we didn't go to Cancun knowing it was Spring Fever or whatever it's called. Dolores made the travel plans, and I love her but she's clueless. Honestly, both Maddie and me didn't know either. We're all close to 60 and what do we know about college kids and sus loquerias? So, off we go to Cancun on a dream vacation. But this ain't no bucket list story. Nobody's dying or desperate that way. We just wanted to relax and slide into this part of our lives. We been friends forever, and I don't care if my daughter thinks they're tacky and déclassé or whatever. These women have been through thick and thin with me, and they've been more supportive than she will ever be. We gonna be there for each other until only one of us is standing—and I hope to God it isn't me. 'Cause I won't have anybody left.

My daughter once saw pictures of us when we were younger in a photo album. She laughed and made fun of us hippies. We *were* hippies, so what? We were young and carefree and believed the world could be changed. Shoot us. How the hell she get so cynical? So freaking conservative? She must take after her goddamn father, that puto who's never even given her a dime. No one demanded that jerk marry me, but he could have manned up and be a father to her. All I got was complaints about being illegitimate after she found out what that meant in that dictionary I bought her for her twelfth birthday.

Since we're on the subject of the "father," let me make something clear. I will never forgive him for telling her about my plans for the abortion, on one of a handful of times that bastard even talked to her. That's just how mean and spiteful he is. But she couldn't see that. She couldn't take my side. She took the word of a man who knocked me up and abandoned us both. She prefers to harp on the one thing that made me seem wicked and selfish. She couldn't consider my financial situation at the time. The fear in my heart that I couldn't be a good mother. That I was a young woman trying to figure out my life and then having the responsibility to care for another.

I wasn't ready. Maybe the fact I'm talking like this 38 years later tells me I was right. But I didn't abort her. And from her, the college-educated liberal who talks up a storm about the right to choose, I don't need the flak and guilt. Monsita has said many abusive things to me, but when she found out and screamed that being aborted would have been better than having me as her mother, she 125 knocked it outta the park. A grand slam. But that's just rough waters under the bridge.

When we got to the resort, we saw all these young people. Three AARP members in the middle of these tanned half-naked bodies. Dolores and I were not happy having to walk around in one-piece bathing suits with those kids around. Maddie, of course, still looks pretty good in a swimsuit. She works out, runs, the whole nine yards. She's always been hot. Men have always swarmed around her like she's the last Coke in the desert.

I want to put this out there because don't think for a moment the woman in that video was doing something to get her cookies off. I say this because all my adult life she's considered me a slut. I mean, she wouldn't say that to my face—mainly because I'd slap her, but she's thought it. Oh, for sure. Her generation, so cool about sex and all, like they invented it. If it wasn't for us, they'd all be virgins messed up from lack of screwing. My mom never talked to me about menstruation. When it happened, and I freaked, she handed me a box of sanitary napkins. That's it.

I couldn't go out with boys. Girls were wearing minis and shorts, and I was walking around with long dresses and unshaven legs. Someday, they said, I'd meet a nice boy at church and get married. Until then, no intimate relations. My parents made me pray to get rid of impure thoughts. One day, I made the mistake of bringing a *Playgirl* into my house. I had borrowed it from a friend at school. I knew my mother checked my room all the time. She was like a Puerto Rican gestapo. But I thought she wouldn't check a little corner of my closet. When she found it, she went ballistic. Had me face the corner, kneeling on grains of rice, and praying for hours. That wasn't the worst, though. My father couldn't look at me for weeks. Kids today should thank us every day they don't have the stupidity and ignorance about sex we faced. It's not in Monsita or her generation to thank anybody for anything. They're all ingrates who think the world owes them everything and anything.

I had many men, so what? Most of them I enjoyed because I learned to love my body. I learned to enjoy an orgasm. To her, that seems—what she call it? A "dated notion." Yeah, well back then it was a freakin' monumental world-shattering breakthrough. What the hell. We learned what an orgasm was! I loved my curves and did not want to be an anorexic twig. As a Puerto Rican woman, I was proud of my butt. She, on the other hand. Don't get me started on the Puerto Rican thing. I knew I had lost my daughter when she started complaining about inheriting her ass from me. Oh, my God! You should pray to the Gods of Sex that you have a beautiful, full, round shapely ass. She wanted to be like those flat-assed white girls in college.

That's when I knew she was lost. But that wasn't new, really. 'Cause she's always been ashamed of her culture and people. That's why she changed her name, the one I gave her. Didn't like Ramona. Didn't like being called Monsita. I wanted to share my life with her … Sorry, excuse me. Thanks for the tissue. I get emotional, sometimes. Anyway … That's why I named her after me. 'Cause it was only me and her. I was passing not only a name but a family history. My grandmother was Ramona. I was proud to have her name because she was strong and fought for her children, my mother included, who was also Ramona. I thought she'd understand. That she'd be proud, too. Guess I was wrong. She said kids at school always made fun of her "hicky spicky" name. She dreamed to be called Brittany and go by Brit, so she went and changed it legally.

You know how much that hurt me? No big deal, she said, shrugging one shoulder, like she had just taken a dump. That was the most ignorant thing she ever said to me. She's never understood the ethnic thing. I see that now. Never understood what it means to be Puerto Rican. She and the other millennials. How much we've struggled so that her generation can succeed. How much we keep struggling. And how does she repay us? By giving her people and culture the finger. I tried to educate her, but obviously it's another thing I failed at. It's not surprising she married Greg Spengler, The Whitest Man On Earth, who probably has Nazi tendencies. And that she moved to the suburbs to live the "ideal" life. Not surprising either that I was the only one from our family invited to the wedding. Me and Marvin, my brother, who didn't show up. He was always the smart one. And do you know she sat me with her friends and co-workers. Had the nerve to tell me, I thought you'd like that, mom. They're from New York. Yeah. That's my daughter.

We didn't go to Cancun to whore our old bodies, you know. We minded our business, tried to stay away from those crazy kids. They too wild! Drinking and puking everywhere. Having sex everywhere. Jumping into pools from balconies. Drugs, smoking pot. Sometimes running naked down the boulevard. Shameful. Like Sodom and Gomorrah by the beach. You probably thinking I'm a hypocrite for saying that because I had a wild life myself. Yeah, I drank a bit, smoked, and popped a few pills. But I'm clean now.

My daughter doesn't like hearing about me finding Jesus, but it's the truth. I'm not some fanatic preaching all over the place. I come from a religious family, but you don't really understand a spiritual life when you're young and rebellious. When you want worldly things and hormones dominate your thoughts and feelings. I had a rough life she puts me down for and then I find something to lead me to inner peace and she mocks me. "Religious methadone," she called it. That I had found another addiction to add to my list. I cleaned up a long time ago, rid myself of my demons. I'm in a spiritual place but she can't see that. She can't say, Mom, I'm happy for you. There's no winning with her. Sometimes, you try but your kids end up being jerks. That's God's honest truth.

I'm saying this because the entire scene in Cancun was perverse. The tipping point was that contest with those young girls, some underage I bet, with the wet T-shirts. Taking them off to win a gift card. And that slimy guy videotaping it. Maddie and Dolores wanted a drink, and I tagged along to have sparkling water by the pool. We were sitting there like I said minding our own business and the circus began. Sat through the silly hip-hop, with guys' pants halfway down their asses, and girls in bikinis grinding up against them. Listened to the emcee's lame sex jokes. Watched them shoot tees out of those guns. Bored out of our gourd, but too tired to get up and move through the crowds of stinky, sweaty, drunk bodies.

Then they brought out the Kim Kardashian wannabes in the T-shirts. Well, I couldn't take it no more. I thought back on my life and how these girls were going in the same direction. It's hard enough for women without these bastards taking advantage. I know what it's like to want affection so bad it makes you stupid. To need men to validate you. I made many mistakes. Don't get me wrong. I was discovering my body and sexuality. But I was ignorant about how to go about it. I wanted to share, not be used. I didn't finish college, but I learned a thing or two from the classes I took. I've read.

I just started boiling, seeing these men, especially the middle-aged ones pawing these women, shouting nasty things at them, and poor things so drunk out of their minds smiling and strutting like bimbos. They were losing any shred of decency and integrity they had. It doesn't have to be like that. They had choices but they had no clue they did.

Then these guys started chanting at them to strip and take off their T-shirts. The emcee announced the start of the Bouncing Boobilicious Boob Contest. All three of us were disgusted. About fifteen girls sashayed on the stage all smiles and giggles. When the emcee told them to take off their tops, I got up and made my way to the stage. Maddie and Dolores followed me, asking me where I was going.

I elbowed and pushed, getting nasty looks and the foulest language I have ever heard. There's no respect for seniors anymore. I didn't understand half what they said, but it sounded raunchy enough to make me blush. They shoved and tussled me, but I got on that stage and started yelling at the emcee, the organizers, the audience, everyone. Maddie looked at me like I was nuts. Dolores grabbed my hand to get me off the stage. Come on, dearie, she tells me, it isn't worth it.

I don't know what pushed me over. I think it was that stupid emcee, putting his lips together, throwing kisses, and humping the air. I screamed, You wanna see tits, and took off my top. There were groans. Some of those stupid bitches shouted ewwwww. That's when Dolores yelled back at them, something like, Take a good look 'cause that's what they're gonna be like down the line, honey. One of them shouted back, Shut the fuck up, granny. So then Dolores took her top off and started jumping up and down. Maddie said what the hell and she stripped too. GILF, someone shouted and there was this huge cheer. I kept yelling to stop abusing young women and then these muscled guys came over and dragged us out. That really pissed us all. We kicked and punched them. I think Dolores bit one of them. They had no right to treat us like that. That son-of-bitch emcee yells, Give it up for the grannies, like it was part of the show. Then they played that dumb song about letting the dogs out.

We didn't know they were recording that part. They had a great time with it. Calling it "Grannies Gone Wild." They said it's gone viral. When Maddie showed it to me, I was shocked. I can't believe they'd put something like that on the internet. But I'm just telling you there was a reason why we did it. Like everything else in my life that seems strange and embarrasses my daughter. And like always she will not see it that way. She'll only see a silly-ass old woman making a fool of herself. That should have known better. Who again has shamed her—like that has been the mission of my life.

Deep down, it's not about the video, is it? ... Maybe, I didn't measure to what she wanted in a mother. Sorry, she can't go back for an exchange or refund. I'm over worrying about our relationship. Done. I refuse to go to my grave feeling guilty about not being a better mother. The selfish, ungrateful child she's always been. Done trying to figure her out. Trying to win her over. Tired of being blamed for every little problem in her life. The hell with that. I'm just too exhausted to deal with this crap. I'm not waiting for the conversation, which will begin with, So, you want to explain yourself? To which, I say, be happy in your ideal life, my sweet daughter. I wish the best for you and Addie. No need for you to call, text, or email, or whatever. Just let me live my life, without having to hear you criticize how I've lived it. How I'm living it. Or, better yet, how I'm going to live it. Because you damn sure can bet, some changes are coming.

INWORLD

HIS WIFE OF TWENTY-SIX years died, and he couldn't get around to slipping the ring off his finger. I should, to move on, I know, he would tell friends, shrugging and smiling. But I just can't. He started wearing the ring on the alternate hand as a halfway measure; the white, circular tan line visible on his left. He twirled it for minutes, while he talked or streamed television, never looking at the ring once. Sometimes, he'd stare at their wedding picture: two young happy people, dressed in standard nuptial formal wear, the hairstyles and Marvin's beard dating them as millennial newlyweds. In the picture Ann Marie, a plump blonde with a broad, pale face, smiles into the camera.

Ann Marie hardly complained about anything, had been blessed with health for most of her life. She thought the pain would go away, didn't think about seeing a doctor until the pain reached unbearable levels and her eyes and skin turned yellow. Less than a year ago, the doctors diagnosed the pancreatic cancer and started immunotherapy. Marvin recounted the visits to the hospital, the moments helping her in and out of the bathroom as she puked or after the diarrhea. Seeing her fade, as she became gaunt with hollow cheeks, her lively blue eyes larger than usual. She died seven months after the diagnosis.

By his own admission, Marvin was a simple man who didn't waste time thinking about things. He just wanted to forget this blow in his life by regaining a sense of routine. But he'd come home and the unexpected silence in the house felt weird. At first, he would blurt out something that happened at the post office as he walked through the door, expecting Ann Marie's sarcastic response. At night, he continued to sleep on his half side of the bed. With time, the house relinquished every trace of her scent. He found fewer hairs stranded on his T-shirts.

Her presence. The sense she was looking at him without looking at her or humming while doing some chore somewhere in the house. The face he knew she made when talking to one of the kids on the phone in another room. The footprints she left across the floor after coming out of the tub. All that, and more, disappeared. That was when he understood he was alone.

Meals were the hardest. Not only because he degenerated from Ann Marie's wonderful dishes to microwavable cuisine. For close to three decades his wife sat across from him at the table, and they talked about daily events in their lives. They shared small-town gossip, laughed about funny past moments, discussed the latest about the kids and grandkids. Planned their future. It got to the point he hated to sit down and eat. They always made it a point to have a sit-down dinner. Even after the kids were gone. Marvin had gotten too used to it. He finally decided to eat in the family room while watching TV. Until then, he ate in the dining room, seated at a table for eight, feeling like the only one at the kids' table.

The silence coaxed memories to surface. He'd think back to a younger Annie, when they were dating. Or how they'd clean the dishes together after supper, talking some more. Now, he stared at the greasy plastic microwave container, panned the furniture, the forgotten pictures on the wall. Got to the point he couldn't stand listening to the digital wall clock tick. He started playing music after that, anything to break the cemetery feeling in the house.

It took a while before he invited someone over. Mike, his best friend and only company. Both served in the Air Force at the local base. Later, they both landed jobs at the Lakeville post office. Each was the other's Best Man. Marvin knew Mike was happy to see his friend being more sociable again, after all the days coming to work haggard, eyes puffy from sleepless nights and crying, clothes unkempt and sometimes stained with Ann Marie's vomit. After she died, he just wasn't himself. He hardly talked, which was unusual, and he had always been smiling and laughing, which Mike told him was at odds with his face—those lean lips and small, brown eyes overlaid with thick, droopy eyelids that made him look dour. At the post office, he had always been chatty and open with everyone, and nothing seemed too private or taboo. When he turned sullen and took too many mental days, it became a worry for everyone. Going postal is not just a catchy phrase for people working in the post office.

It was a hot August day and Marvin opened another two pale ales. They had just finished watching a Red Sox game. He slid a cigarette out of the pack with two yellowish fingers.

So, have you started going out again? Mike asked.

Marvin took a long drag and pumped out smoke rings.

Nah, can't get into it. That's a whole production, I feel. 'Sides— go where? Lakeville isn't exactly rockin'. And driving downtown to a bar full of wasted college kids? No thanks.

To be honest, he continued, been surfin' the porn sites. Checked them out while married, not gonna lie. But occasionally. 'Cause, Annie and me got it on. Never had a problem in that department. He threw a smiling glance to the side.

You turning perv on us, Marv?

Screw you, Mike. I'm talking normal stuff. He pointed his cigarette at his friend. Let me make that clear right now. Anyways, yeah, I went on and got myself hot and whacked off. He raised his right hand. Guilty.

His friend laughed.

Hell, what else am I supposed to do?

Nah, I hear you, man. It's been rough for you.

Marvin sat, looking nowhere, slouched against the sofa. He raised his thick eyelids.

Annie did this funny thing after making love, he said. Wrapped her right leg around the base of my back, near my butt, while she held on to my head. Sometimes we fell asleep that way. That's better than sex, any day. He sucked the beer suds and crushed his cig. Well, almost, he added, grinning.

One day, after hours of browsing, he decided to enter InWorld, a site Mike told him about. He didn't know what to expect; didn't go to the website with any expectations. It was a typical, impulsive web visit. He was bored, running out of things to do online, and he googled and found the site. He had never heard of virtual worlds until he and Mike were chatting about this and that, usual stuff, during the sort. Then Mike started talking about a movie where people lived through robots they controlled from their homes.

Sky's the limit with these robots, he told Marvin. You're young and sexy forever in a world where you can be free and wild.

Sure, Mike, Marvin said, it's a world called Hollywood.

Hey, it's not far from reality, he said. Look at InWorld.

Marvin had no clue, and Mike returned his dumb expression with a sigh, like his friend was the biggest moron in the world. Mike knew about all the computer cyber stuff, read a lot of sci-fi and probably had seen every possible sci-fi movie ever made. But even after explaining it to him, Marvin didn't understand. He filed it under "curious but who cares" and got on with real life.

The website opened to a promo where you board a hover craft that flies through various places. Pixilated beautiful vistas of forests, mountains, beaches, deserts, international cities, the Wonders of the World, that looked like so real he thought he was viewing a travel ad. That's followed by a montage of people partying, dancing, kissing, hanging out, having a great time. With a smile, an amazingly realistic looking female avatar offered an invitation.

Adventure and opportunity await you InWorld … Begin your new life now … The catch was that he had to buy a headset and special gloves. It was a bit steep and he thought about it. Days passed, but he kept returning to the promo, lingering over it, wondering if it could possibly be that real.

When he opened the package, he couldn't believe how small and light the headset was. It resembled a pair of sunglasses with a plastic strap that hugged your head. He hardly felt it on his head. The gloves lighter than your winter ones. Pressing a few buttons on the headset and gloves, his surroundings disappeared, and he suddenly transported into another space. A female avatar explained how to begin and then he found himself facing a floating screen with options for his avatar. He selected a rugged male avatar and named it Mark Cavatelli, because that's what he had for dinner. Once completed, he marveled at how every part of it looked real. From the small hairs on his hands to the textures of the clothing. Before, it seemed like he was a floating head, now he sensed an attachment to a body. He wiggled his fingers, jumped up and did a little dance. He fumbled to walk without bumping into objects, trying to learn how to navigate around the field of view.

Once he learned how to transport to sims, he began exploring. The attention to detail in the design, the beauty of the created landscapes, was impressive, sometimes breathtaking. Where they lived was so damn cold in the winter that the sim beaches naturally attracted him. The times he had visited family in Puerto Rico with Annie, when it was still part of the US, they spent so much time at the beach that both got bad sunburns. He loved hanging out on an InWorld beach lounger, listening to the music he streamed, and scanning the area. The salty smell of ocean, sea birds gawking overhead, grains of sand stuck to his body. It was like being in a real beach.

At one beach, he got a message to lose his clothing or wear beach wear. He had transported to a nude beach, and a strict sim manager attached a big sign above him announcing to the world his violation. He panned around and saw naked avatars. Every male avatar had tanned muscular bodies with ripped abs and was anatomically accurate. After taking his clothes off, a feat requiring slow instruction and frustration, he discovered his naked avatar resembled Ken, as in Ken and Barbie.

Marvin covered where his privates should have been. A Foxy Gold sent him a message: Looks like someone's missing their hardware. When he spotted Foxy, it was a shocking discovery. There she was in her birthday suit, with bouncy breasts and butt, wavy blonde hair, and sparkling, big green eyes. She even had tan lines. He couldn't believe someone could put together a computer-generated replica of a human being like that. In comparison, his looked like a child's cartoon drawing of a person. He scrambled for the exit button and logged out.

The next day, he re-entered the virtual world and researched the anatomical possibilities of an InWorld avatar, which first led him to freebie sims, where designers dumped much of their junk as a marketing ploy. He was willing to accept any type of gift. Until he saw how cheap it looked compared to others. Marvin didn't want to walk around with a cartoonish avatar sporting a penis that resembled a digital representation of a dildo. He found out soon enough that like in real life, you get what you paid for, so he purchased some InWorld currency. He spent the entire evening jumping from one sim to another, buying a new and improved look for his virtual mini-me.

Through the magic of CGI and Marvin Correa's imagination, the updated Mark Cavatelli was digitally spawned into InWorld. He was tanned, broad chested, and tall like most avatars. Long, black flexi-hair framed a handsome face sporting a stubbly beard. His blue eyes markedly different from Marvin's brown. He looked like a male character on a romance novel cover.

He hesitated to buy a penis. He visited several sim stores—even a special mall to buy one—and looked at boards with pictures of huge ones, advertising different types and prices, and he had to laugh. It was stupid and strange. Embarrassing, even. Once he got over the initial awkwardness, it was like buying a pair of sneakers or fishing pole or, more to the point, condoms at the drugstore. He shopped everywhere and then came across one that looked amazingly real. Marvin was overjoyed.

On a break, Mike asked, What was your first InWorld sex experience like?

Marvin sat back, pulled out a cigarette but didn't light it right away. He laughed, sipped his coffee, took a drag, and shook his head.

Her name was Minnie Morpork. Met her at some club playing trance music. Brought her back to my apartment in virtual New Orleans. Finally realized you need a place of your own InWorld, if anything to have a place to dress, and you know, I've always loved the Big Easy. Anyway, we get to my place and she jumped on me. Had me doing all kinds of things to her. She's chatting away, telling me all kinds of nasty things. "Stick your tongue in there, yeah," or "Bang me hard like a slut," stuff like that. She came and, poof, left before I did. Felt kinda used, to tell you the truth.

Not even a cuddle, huh? You went back after that?

Did you give up after your first lame lay with Margery Mason?

Jeez, that was high school.

Don't matter. You were a virgin, and in InWorld so was I.

Seriously, Marv?

Okay, so I was curious. And it felt—I don't know—liberating. Anything goes, and there's a shortage of fucks to give. I tried stuff I'd never do for real.

The sims Marvin visited those first months of exploration ranged from raunchy meat markets to trendy clubs or exclusive brothels. A slice of InWorld dedicated to licentiousness or sin, depending on how you looked at it. Like the nude beaches, where people pranced around exhibiting their privates. Each one with its own secluded areas for sexual play. Or dance clubs, which had good, sometimes live, music and were enjoyable just to chill and dance, and served as pickup joints.

Marvin wondered sometimes if Mike wished he had never mentioned InWorld. Most days, he couldn't close his big mouth during the morning sort, complaining how InWorld pole dancers enticed you to watch them and tried to con you into giving them money. He elaborated on his meetings with the occasional escort. What's the point of that? I told them. I ain't paying in real life, not gonna start in any virtual life. Mike said huh. Right, told one, Why pay? So many people just do it for free here. And she told me, it's the difference between getting the steak or the wrapper. I'm the steak, she said. He laughed and elbowed Mike.

During lunchtime, he'd continue. Last night, I visited a place called Bimbo Land. For real, he said, responding to his friend's incredulous laugh. That's what they called themselves. They have enormous boobs, outrageous big lips, ridiculously huge butts. They resemble giant love dolls, I kid you not. Mike shook his head, maybe about the bimbos, maybe about him. Marvin didn't care. Their leader, Raegina Dentata, he said, wore pink latex and matching kinky boots. She wore a head dress that looked like an upside-down butt. And she carried this staff with three spirals at the top.

She told me, In this land, men are our guests, but they must do as we say. You must give yourselves to the Bimbos.

Why not? So, they undressed me and led me to a temple. All this time, there was this singing. It was this beautiful, sad melody. I didn't understand the words, but I couldn't stop listening. When the music ended, Raegina stared down into my face.

Would you like to try the Convertatron? she said. She pointed to a spinning black-and-white spiral. It will transform you, she said.

How?

It depends on you, she told me. That's the fun part. And she started laughing.

What else you got?

We can motorboat you until you surrender.

They laid me on a marble slab, and they did, every one of them. With those humongous breasts. My face took a beating, and I cried for them to stop after a few minutes.

Then Raegina yelled, Power to the boobs! The others answered, May they rule! And they kept chanting that way. Louder and louder.

They went into a frenzy and danced around me, raising their arms, and gyrating their breasts and butts. It freaked me out, and I transported myself the hell out of there.

The Bimbos led to other stories. About the crazy avatars wielding bats and striking people. The pregnant women, and the ones with babies. The angry woman who got a kick out of teasing men hitting on her. The bikini clad woman calling out the InWorld "bitches and sluts." The endless procession of Walking Penises—male AV's with perpetual erections—and their female counterparts, the Naked Nymphos.

One woman flashing an erect boner wanted to do him. Ah, ain't gonna happen, sweetheart, he told her. Then she started humping him.

You got your fancy types, he told Mike. If they IM you, ninety percent chance you gonna get laid. Like this one I met at a jazz club where you gotta go all dressed up. She came on to me, looking fantastic in this fancy gown and took me back to her mansion on an island. I mean, this house had like gazillion rooms, the swimming pool, Jacuzzi, a Porsche parked in the driveway. She held my hand and walked me to a yacht by her dock. There, she stripped, and turned into a wild woman. She screamed things that made me blush.

That was weird, man. Not the weirdest, though. Not even close. There was this Afrodite Nerlman, a BDSM type. Now, I'm not into that kink. InWorld, after a while, you say what the hell and try anything. It isn't real, right? And what happens InWorld, stays InWorld. Mike said huh. Maybe, Marvin said, the Goth look I had going on attracted her, who knows. So, I find myself paddling her, and she's yelling, You're my master. *Please* punch me. I mean, how polite can you get? I gotta tell you, Mike, I'm not that guy. I kissed her instead, 'cause deep down I'm a romantic. She freaked out. Why you being nice to me? she asked. Then, piff, gone.

On any typical day, he picked up something to eat at a drive-thru and drove home excited to immerse himself in the fantasy. For months, Marvin explored every corner of the virtual world, mostly wandering through the sexual confines of its digital boundaries. Other times, exploring other possibilities. He joined a vampire coven, then quit. Too much drama, he said. It was like high school all over again. Then a pack of Lycans. The avatar was cool, he admitted, but that also grew old. Fought zombies, dragons, and dinosaurs. Lived in a cyberpunk society and ancient Rome.

He visited fun places like the amusement parks or special theme sites. Checked out the educational sims, the museums, the dance clubs and music venues. Even dropped in on a salsa club. He had never done that in real life. Growing up, there wasn't music in the house, unless it was religious. Ramona, his sister, used to sneak off to the clubs in New York, always lying that she was going to study or something else. She tried to teach him how to dance salsa, but

he was hopelessly bad. When he moved upstate, he became a fan of country, bluegrass, and rock. Ramona used to make fun of his redneck tastes in music. So, when he entered Club Coqui, it was a new world.

The music was intense and loud. Colorful neon palm trees everywhere. Behind the DJ table, a gigantic coqui—the country's beloved tiny frog—smiled and winked. Everyone sat at tables shaped like the island. The avatars packing the floor danced tightly, spinning like beautiful figurines. He smiled as he remembered his sister's frustration in trying to teach him the steps. Poor Monsie, he thought. The many times he stepped on her feet. On one session, she wore Doc Martens. Even with the clunky shoes, she showed more skill than he could ever have. How can you be a Rican and not have any rhythm? she'd said. Like this, she'd shout, grabbing his hips and shaking them for him. It wasn't like he didn't want to learn. He often wished that he could because it looked like fun, and the couples were so graceful.

Hey, this is InWorld, he thought. I only need to ask a partner to dance and with a few screen taps, we're on the floor. So, he asked a few women, and they declined. Too much like real life. Maybe he wasn't dressed properly. He had on a pair of jeans, shirt, and loafers. The women wore evening dresses or elegant slacks and tops. And bling everywhere. The guys had jackets or slacks rather than denim. He searched his inventory and changed.

A brunette in a green dress sat alone at a table, so he asked her. I don't dance with gringos, she said. He almost corrected her but held back. Why should he? He didn't need to defend his ethnicity to anyone. Besides, he understood Puerto Ricans harbored ill-will toward Americans, even after independence. He had family with similar sentiments. He scanned the club. Everyone was chatting in Spanish, and he couldn't make out everything being said. Even if he could dance, the vibe wasn't there. Could he even have a decent conversation if he had a partner? He noticed he was the whitest-looking avatar in the place.

Instead of transporting out, he decided to take a walk outside. The club was in virtual San Juan. Walking the blue ballast streets of the historic sector of the city brought back memories of the few times he had visited the real capital, back when the island was called Puerto Rico. The colorful houses lining these narrow-simulated streets were faithful to the originals. The air was sultry, and he could hear the music emanating from the club. He crossed the Plaza de Armas. To him, it seemed a replica. The fountain in the middle, the green kiosks, the benches and trees lining the plaza, the surrounding shops. They even had the multitude of pigeons. Was it like he remembered it so long ago? Or were his memories too distant and estranged?

He left virtual San Juan and never returned.

One day it hit him. Whatever pleasure he was getting from these virtual erotic escapades was not enough. They could be intense and gratifying, sometimes incredibly so. He had read on the InWorld blogs how the sexual roleplay wrapped people in an emotional and psychological bonding that, by most accounts, is genuinely intimate, keenly arousing, and passionate. He had experienced that at times.

One night, he casually entered InWorld, transported to one of his usual haunts, found a woman and brought her to his new condo, fully furnished with the most advanced toys. He doesn't remember her name, but she was pretty. Curly blond hair, falling to her shoulders. Plush, glossy lips that broke into a sly smile. She was not afraid to own an avatar with curves. He appreciated that. Her cornflower blue eyes had seized him the moment he saw her at the club.

It was more romantic than most outings. Lots of kissing, caressing, holding. The sex was slow, deliberate, meant to linger and enjoy. When she left, he logged and shut down the system. He straightened his pants, zipped up. Then settled back into the recliner and smoked a cigarette. Surrounded by cigarette smoke and darkness, Marvin heard the silence in his home.

What am I doing? What was I thinking? That kept repeating in his head. He didn't want to hook up with anyone from InWorld. A few people did that. But he was a widower, and he thought most of the women he met in InWorld, if they were even women, would recoil if they saw his real appearance. This virtual world presented a stage where Marvin could only be an actor, forever.

All along, I knew it was fake, even when it felt real, he confessed to Mike. They were at their favorite watering hole drinking on a Friday, after bowling. But it started feeling too real, you know what I mean? I don't know, he said, his face contorted with confusion. It seemed unnatural to love something like that so much. Mike listened, partly relieved, but also saddened for his friend.

Got to the point *I* started feeling fake, Marvin said, not just my avatar, but me, my entire life, everything around me. The only thing not fake were the people behind the avatars. He took a sip of beer and smiled. People are the same, Mike, very real, even in a fake world. There are serious people, funny types, brainy geeks, greedy people, sex addicts, posers, artsy folks, all types. Even when anything goes, some can't let go. They won't shed their fake clothing in a sim beach. They're embarrassed by the sex. Others hide behind their avatars. They use the fantasy and freedom to be insensitive, cruel assholes.

Marvin avoided InWorld, started hanging out with friends. One night, Mike set him up with Sheila, a widow a few years younger than he. She worked at the nearby college with Mike's wife, Stephanie. Mike and Stephanie suggested a double date and, ignoring the bad high school vibe over such an outing, he met them at an Italian restaurant.

At first glance, Sheila was a pleasant enough woman. Slender, not bad looking. Shoulder-length brown hair, obviously bleached. She had a tight smile, as Marvin remembered, and upon a closer look wrinkles that gave away not only her age but her sad life. The evening was enjoyable, without any spectacularly awkward moment, so they decided to continue seeing each other. It didn't last long.

Sheila is one of the saddest people I've ever met, Marvin told Mike. I liked her, really, I did. And God knows, I'm lonely. But she hardly smiled or laughed, that woman. She carried this grief with her, everywhere she went, you know? And she wouldn't open up about it, whatever it was. We went out a few times. Typical stuff, 143 dinner, movie, drinks. Nothing interested her. After one night of drinking, we came back to my house and had a go at it. It was like we were both virgins again. She was as stiff as a board. Her skin felt like thin paper to me. She was trembling and cold. Painful for her, cause, you know, not enough lubrication. I couldn't keep it up. He laughed and shook his head. We didn't finish. It was kinda pathetic.

After staring at his hands on the table for a few seconds, he said: She just made me sad, Mike, and I had enough of that. I wanna be happy. I wanna laugh and die laughing. He tapped his box of cigs on the table a couple of times. Nothing there for me but emptiness. I hate to say this, but I got off more on InWorld.

After the Sheila episode, he brooded. Watched TV. Bowled a bit. Went deer hunting with the guys. Visited his daughter, Alison, downstate in Albany a few times; his son, Chris, down in the Bronx. Chris's Bronx was gentrified, with Starbucks and fancy restaurants sprouting everywhere for the recently arrived hipster "settlers." He had blurry memories of his childhood Bronx, which ran through his mind like a bad ghetto flick. He grew up there when neighborhoods resembled bomb sites and drugs were easier to find than an open library.

After joining the Air Force right out of high school, he was stationed at the air base upstate. That's where he met Annie. He married her and that's when the problems with the family began. His mother never accepted Annie. Complained that she was too fat, made fun of her paleness and her small teeth. Thought she wasn't good enough for him. Criticized the "indecent" clothes she wore. Every time he brought her to visit was like jumping from a plane without a parachute into a minefield. It was always awkward because they couldn't communicate. His parents spoke little English and Annie didn't know a word of Spanish. He hated having to translate everything, or worse having his sister Ramona mangle the meaning of everything. Annie had a proud streak to her, too. It's not my fault, they don't speak English, she would tell Marvin.

The big blow-up came when Alison was born. Annie wanted to baptize her in a Catholic church. His parents were strict Pentecostals who believed Catholicism was a false religion, that their followers, mundanos, are not of the spiritual world. Annie got her way and no one from the family came up for the baptism. That upset his wife, who felt no matter the issues they had, family should stick together. Damn, that's their grandchild, Marv, she told him. He couldn't argue with her. He never looked back to the city, or his family. Marvin's parents retired to the island and moved into what Annie called a shack. The last time he saw them was when he visited Puerto Rico and spent most of the time at the beach.

The family referred to him as El Gringo, but he didn't give a damn one way or the other. His son updated him on the family drama he didn't care to hear. The latest gossip had to do with Ramona's recent squabble with her daughter Brit. Chris couldn't believe his father hadn't seen the video with his aunt dancing half-naked. You must be the only person in the world who hasn't seen it, Dad. Marvin shrugged. His sister was always wild. The entire family was a bunch of lunatics. The happiest moment in his life was when he left for the Air Force.

He would come back from those family trips drained, in a funk and lonely. To keep himself busy, he returned to an old hobby of building car models. The latest, a '52 Eldorado. He did that for a while, hanging up his collectibles on shelves he cleared of past family memories. That couldn't kill enough time between work and routine chores to deaden the deepening silence swallowing him. At Mike's insistence, he hung out a couple of nights at a new local bar with other guys from the post office. That got stale after a while, especially when he would end up alone at the bar, watching guys go home to wives or with girls they picked up.

Eventually, he logged on again. He had been watching TV and nothing caught his attention. He flipped channels like a zombie and turned the damn thing off. Slouching on the couch, he stared at the headset and wondered how things were InWorld. How his virtual friends were doing. If any new sims had sprung up. He had re-entered with the idea of giving his avatar a complete makeover. New skin for Mark, new shape, clothes, hair, new everything. He hit the adult sims again but soon grew tired of them, and probably would have left for good, if he hadn't met a lovely, friendly blonde, Cindy.

Together, they shared a big house in a resort. On the weekends, Mark threw parties for his InWorld friends and neighbors. Today found him grilling burgers and franks while talking to his best friend, Rick. Rick Montana had served in the Air Force, and his folks were Puerto Rican. They had both those things in common, but they met at a motorcycle racing event. Cindy floated in the pool, sunbathing, and chatting with Lou's wife, Gina. The Montanas had kids InWorld, something that Mark and Cindy had discussed. Their kids were splashing water in the pool.

Hey, cut it out, Gina yelled. Oh, they're only kids, let them have fun, Cindy said. Gina stared at her. You must never have had kids in real life. It's the same here, believe me.

Mark grabbed two beers from an icy cooler. He slid into a lounger next to Rick, handed him one. Out toward the mountains, the Arizona sunset brought spectacular colors. Burnt orange mixed with yellow and purple. He breathed deep and took in the warm, desert air. He sat back and let the sun and beer drift him into that hazy serenity he loved. Cindy waved to him and he threw her a kiss. He held out the bottle to Rick. To life, he said.

RUNWAY RUNAWAY

THIS IS THE THIRD time he's had to resew, and she's had to hear about it. She wants to hurt him every time he sighs and rolls his eyes. Then Mika starts getting on her case. Because she's lost a few pounds. *Bitch, you're my agent, not my therapist.* She's sick of working to keep up her plenitude. Tired of having to eat all those carbs. If she had to eat another bowl of pasta, she would puke. The other day, she had to insist on skipping dessert just one day. Please, dear god, no more cake and ice cream. The next outfit draws her attention. It's a fab summer dress, she says out loud, caressing its texture, holding it up in awe.

She's thinking, fine, you're the man. But do your effin' job so I can do mine. I'm here to walk it down the runway and make it come alive. 'Cause at the end of the day, it's just fabric shaped into a dress that needs my curves to make it dance. Needs my 'tude and style to sell it. Everyone needs to step back and let me work the magic.

Just stitch and shut up, 'kay? she snaps at the designer. Yes, I've lost a few pounds, shoot me.

Don't tempt me, he says. Now go—you're on. Then, he throws the eye-rolling shade. Has the nerve to push her toward the catwalk. So, she turns around and slaps him, harder than maybe she wanted. Yeah, she slapped Zaló, the God of Couture. In front of his ass kissers, the photographer, the other models, her agent, business associates, and friends. He's steaming, about to go off on one of his infamous meltdowns, but she's not having it. She's all professional and sashays toward the runway. And she's killing the dress. Backstage, she knows he's watching and loving his creation come alive as her body moves. His anger washes away knowing the media attention this collection will get. She can hear the dollar signs kachinking in his head.

While she struts down the catwalk, she's thinking how she hates this show. Hates the runway set design. Hates Zaló. Hates the entire business. The audience following her like a collective stalker. At the end of the U ramp, she doesn't stop or turn. Instead, she jumps off and keeps going. They think it's Lupi Correa rattling the cage as usual. They clap. In awe, a critic yells her next vlog headline: She's extending the runway! She marches out the door. Behind her, a multitude sheepishly follows. She takes off the heels and tosses them. A bunch of groupies scramble for the prize. She hears slaps and screams. Others stumble and fall. A pile-up. Someone screams, half-crying, Lupi where ya going? She keeps going out the building until she reaches the curb, where she waves a cab to take her home.

She doesn't go home. The few paparazzi assigned to make her life miserable will be there, for sure. Now, with what happened at the show, the rest of the vultures will be there, trying to get a piece of her. She directs the driver to her sister's apartment. Monique lives in Brooklyn by The Barriers. Lupi always has a few clothes stashed there for moments like this. Her sister lives a solitary life. No one suspects she's her sister. She's at work, so Lupi uses her keycard and lets herself in.

After changing into jeans and a tee, she throws a few things into an overnight bag and bounces. Leaves her cell phone with a note to Monique and picks up her extra. The last thing she wants to see are texts and calls blowing up her phone. Her sister knows the deal. She's done this before and will do it again. Or maybe not. Maybe, this might be the last time. Because she's tired of being the show.

The plan is to jet to the island, for peace and tranquility. To escape the madness and stress. She just needs some me-time to recharge and reset. In a flash, she calls the private jet service and schedules a flight to San Juan. At JFK, they pick her up. A few minutes later, she's strapped down on the hypersonic and reaches Albizu Campos airport in an hour. As they land, she sees coastal streets flooded. Dark clouds tell her it's been raining. Once docked, she casually looks out the window. Ocean water has breached the barricades and reaches the workers' knees. A power boat comes to pick up the baggage.

On her way to Customs and Immigration, a large sign welcomes her to the República de Borinquen. The line is thankfully short on the VIP lane. The departure lines are much longer. They're full of young couples with children, seniors in wheelchairs off to the States for a surgery, or students studying abroad. It's getting harder to leave the country. She hands the officer her Boricua passport. He asks if she's a dual citizen, and Lupi nods. One look up from the passport and he stares at her. Excuse me, he says, and calls the office. Lupi purses her lips and looks around. A suit comes out and tells her to follow him. In the office, two of them initiate their game. She opens her purse and hands them $750, American. The price has gone up since last time. Welcome home, one of them says, smiling and counting the money.

First time around, she made a stink and they held her for hours. They took her phone and she couldn't call anyone. They threatened to inform the media that she had been busted with drugs. The officer said this while holding a bag of Changa. So, she paid. Now, they're cool. They have an understanding. It's like she's on their celebrity list. She doesn't come down here often, but with every trip, Lupi hits the lottery. It's only money, a pair of shoes, she thinks. No, not even, because she gets those for free. There's no price she'd pay for peace of mind; that's what she keeps telling herself.

Her Puerto Rican grandparents don't agree on anything, but they both say things have gotten worse since independence. Back in the day, as a colony, it wasn't great either. Once The Change came, the US had its own problems big time, so they dropped PR like a hot potato. This is according to abuelo. They forced independence on us, he says, like they did with citizenship. Turned us citizens because of war. Now, we're a republic because the world is going to hell. Abuela Ramona says it's the "end times." To which her mother always adds, Them end times sure seem endless. One time, Lupi asked her abuelos if they wanted to move to the island. I'll buy each one of you a house, she said. They told her she was crazy. Move there for what? they asked.

Waiting for the helicopter to her villa, she checks her phone for the news. Sure enough, the video of her slapping Zaló and walking out has gone viral. Everyone's wondering where she's at. She shakes her head. World's literally falling apart, and this is news? Life was less complicated back when she was in high school. It didn't matter summer days often were cut short because of the heat. That they had to follow so many rules to conserve water and energy. They found ways to have fun. Like making igloos during winters. Or rowing to friends' houses during floodtimes. Trying to kiss someone with a gas mask was the funniest thing in the world.

Then one day her mom dragged her to the model agency. Thick is in, baby, she tells her, and you got curves. No more scrawny girls modeling. It's like no one can stand skinny people anymore. She made her take the professional name Lupi Correa. Play up your Rican side, she said. Addie Spengler isn't gonna cut it.

One look at her and the agency people fell in love. Stopped everything and signed her up on the spot. It was crazy. She thought it would be good money for college. Never in her wildest dreams did she think it'd go this far. The modeling, the zine spreads, the corp sponsors, her own clothing line, some movie gigs, and her StreamPoetry. Her poetry, which kept her sane. When the big money poured in, there was no time for a degree. But she always loved poetry and kept writing. Mika suggested she post her work on social media. Now, she has five million lovers of her poetry, following her words and fashion style, but now she doesn't have any friends. Or a boyfriend. Her mother made her dump Kevin because he was too skinny. How's that going to look? she said. You, the Queen of Curves, with that slimpy doof? Mika agreed. Ugh, I can see the Twitter threads. No way.

The helicopter arrives and in no time she's landing at her place in Jayuya. She's atop the highest part of the island, where centuries ago the indigenous Tainos lived. Except for the cleaning lady and the gardener, who come once a week, she's alone. She drops her bag and walks to the terrace facing south. Past the muddy brown mountains and yellow lowlands, she spots the olive-green sea. She shivers looking at this view. Feels close to the land, the history flowing through her body. The spirits of the Tainos surround her; she feels them protecting her. Lupi closes her eyes and breathes in deep. A passing whiff smells like burnt roast pork, blending with something metallic and sweet. Then a lingering smell like tanned leather. For an instant, she regrets not bringing her air mask. Covering her nose and mouth, she grabs her bag and rushes into the house.

It's a modest villa. Five bedrooms, three baths, one with a jacuzzi. A spacious living room and huge kitchen, both rarely inhabited. Two enormous walk-in closets, one just for footwear. While here, she spends most of her time in her Lady Lair, in front of her home theater. Or in the bedroom she converted into a recording studio, from where she streams her poetry.

She opens the pantry and laughs. Mika always instructs the cleaning lady to stock it with non-perishables. Boxes of macaroni and cheese, fruit drinks, peanut butter, bags of chips, cookies, and other thickening treats. Without opening the fridge, she visualizes the freezer stacked with quick pasta meals. You would think I pay her by the pound, she thinks.

Lupi sometimes feels that's the case with her. There is so much pressure on her to maintain that fulsome appearance. Lately, she is having doubts. Mika caught her watching the Svelte Movement podcasts and videos, and she went ballistic.

They're just a bunch of Emaciates trying to brainwash you, she said, clicking off the screen.

She stood in front of Lupi, hands on wide hips, owning her own curvy privilege. Then the lecture followed. About how so much was riding on her—like she's a beast of burden.

It's not about you anymore. This she screams, flailing her arms, her eyes cutting through her. Your corporate sponsors have invested millions on you. Millions of fans don't want to see scrawny Lupi Correa. They love the chunky, abundant Lupi. They live a different life through you. One where Meat Days could be any day and access to chocolate is not only for the super-rich. Think of your fans, Lupi. Those poor girls starving for your attention.

Mika doesn't mention young girls stealing food from supermarkets. Parents having to hide bottles of cooking oil so girls won't drink them. That gang of women serving time for breaking into a chocolate factory and hauling off with thousands of boxes. Bakeries have had to hire armed security guards. Lupi has seen the videos of Emaciates crowdfunding for fat injections. Or they're saving to buy fat suits. She gets letters from young girls pleading her to donate fat to them. There are rumors that in the black market a pound of her fat is going for half a million dollars. When Lupi tells Mika that, shocked, her agent pauses and asks, Is that all?

> i'm the runway runaway
> i run to you
> to run with you
> together we'll run into our bodies
> all different and beautiful
> and find our mutual
> love and peace

love your bodies, love yourselves

Lupi Correa sends the poem out, accompanied by a photo of her in couture jogging outfit, with the cutest pink kicks. It starts trending within minutes. She shuts her cell off and turns on the big screen in the home theater. Flips through the news. More dreadful reports about famine, rare diseases, and wars over aquifers. In local news, besides the usual corruption updates, sanitary pipelines, and pump stations bursting; alleged roving bands of cannibals; another hurricane developing off the west coast of Africa.

She flips through entertainment shows, passing on stories about celebrities she knows but dislikes, or those she doesn't know but envies. In fashion news, nothing about her, except the latest StreamPoem. The commentator calls it a whine for help. Mika comes on and tells a reporter that Lupi is taking a few days off to relax. It's been a stressful spring season, she says.

She clicks on the old movie classics channel, flips until *Donnie Darko* pops up. She liked the lead actor, who reminded her of Kevin, her ex. Halfway into the film, she falls asleep.

She sleeps past noon. After eating a light brunch, she takes a blanket and a bottle of lemon water outside. It's cloudy and humid, but an occasional breeze sweeps by. In the distance, crows are cawing. Locals say they have been a nuisance since returning and even attack people. She turns up the raga music and goes through various yoga poses, ending in the lotus. She decides it's an excellent time to smoke the Changa. She prepares the V-Pipe and takes several hits, inhaling deeply.

Before her back touches the blanket, vivid colorful shapes flash toward her and swerve in waves. It feels like she's inside a hyper-fast video game. She becomes acutely aware of the presence of her body. Serenity overtakes her. The music sounds closer, the tabla drum beating against her ear. A ball of white light floats and transforms into a beautiful woman dressed in flowing white robe. Why are you alone, she asks, and Lupi cannot answer. The question saddens her. A spider spirals down, and a lizard waddles across her vision. A dwarf looks at her and laughs, then runs inside the house. Where are you going, she mumbles. Her body floats up, feels movement, as if she were being carried. A mambo plays. The tumbao fills her ears. People surround her, their masked faces peering into her blurry eyes. Their fingers poke her flesh. A woman wears her couture jogging outfit. Everything gets dark. The dwarf chops her leg and waves the bloody stump like a trophy. The masked figures dance around a bonfire, pass the leg around, and bite chunks off. Crows caw in the distance. The woman in her outfit snarls into her face. Lupi stares back. The pink outfit droops on the young woman's emaciated frame. She strikes the same pose as Lupi in her poem photo and laughs. Lupi struggles to lean on her elbow and glares.

Bitch, I wore it better.

THE ADVENTURES
OF MACHO THE DWARF,
OR AN ALLEGORY OF EPIC
PROPORTIONS ABOUT
A LITTLE PERSON

CRISTOBAL, THE CARETAKER OF Porta Coeli, was about to sweep the steps to the entrance of the church, when he saw the bundled baby. The baby was sleeping in an expensive rattan basket, his big head protruding from the beautifully embroidered blanket in which he was tightly wrapped. Cristobal shook his head as if to say, "Another one."

Whenever a woman had a baby she did not want, it appeared here so the Sisters could take it in the orphanage. Most mothers of these children, unable to care for them, took them personally to the convent or the orphanage. From many other similar drops, Cristobal knew that the fine basket, the blanket, and the coloring of this little boy meant a wealthy woman had relations with a dark-skinned man, perhaps a servant, and the well-to-do family had deposited their shame on the doorstep of the church.

As he did with others, Cristobal took the baby to the Dominican Sisters. The Mother Superior didn't even wince or comment anymore. She didn't even take her eyes off her work. She rang a bell summoning Sister Evangeline, who promptly took the baby to the nursery. Undressing the baby and changing him, the Sister noticed the boy's big head and forehead, the shorter limbs, but she didn't make much of it at the time. Pinned to his diaper was a note, standard practice in these cases. The note almost always apologized for abandoning the child, asked the nuns to pray for the wayward mother, and to please take care of the baby who under other circumstances they would have loved and raised.

This one only stated, "Sorry. We can't. His name is Pedro Rico." Its curtness stunned and bothered the nun. She found these notes offensive in their defense of the mothers' reckless and irresponsible sinfulness, but at least they asked for God's mercy. There was always an attempt at contrition, however mangled and insincere. She tried to recall if any young female parishioners had been absent from services to pinpoint the heartless family involved, but she could not. Most likely the family lived in another diocese. As she rocked the sleeping baby, she looked at his dark skin and tiny broad nose and concurred with Cristobal's assessment. Without a doubt, the poor child was being punished for his mother's lustful indiscretion. She shivered and placed baby Pedro in a crib. Later, she took him to the wet nurse when he woke up hungry.

As Pedro matured, it became evident he was a dwarf. This painful realization cast doubt and concern about his future in the convent and beyond its walls. He was now their charge in body and soul, and they could not abandon him like his mother and family. They never had to take care of such a child. They worried that his deformity was Satan's punishment for the mixing of races and would corrupt the other children. The Mother Superior came to the conclusion God was testing them and they had to accept His will. This affirmation, however, did not help Pedro's situation. In fact, it worsened it.

The nuns, even Sister Evangeline, an early ally and protector, distanced themselves from him. They gave him food, the same miserable portions of breadfruit and starchy roots, coupled with an occasional piece of meat or codfish. They provided him shelter, clothed him with tattered rags, and gave him a cot to sleep like the other orphans. But they did not show him the same interest or even the smattering of care and love bestowed on others. Neither did they offer him the same education as the others. They assumed that his physical deformity meant an inability to learn and a lifetime of menial work, so the young dwarf was relegated to doing more chores than the others.

The nuns became adept at finding work suited to his diminutive stature. Pedro became an expert at dusting the convent's crannies; weeding in between thorny bushes; cleaning inside the fireplace ovens; and any other tedious task involving tight space. Pedro's "God-given gift" became a valuable asset for the Sisters, who didn't hesitate to loan him to wealthy members of the congregation in re- turn for contributions to the convent and church. The Dominican priests gave the nuns wine and produce from their garden in exchange for Pedro's services. He was always in demand for theatrical productions that required dressing as a jester. During Christmas, he was loved as baby Jesus. A gentleman from the diocese who reproduced famous paintings of dwarfs kept Pedro busy. The painter had already transformed Pedro into Callot's *Drunken Dwarf*, Molenaer's *Dancing Dwarf*, Bronzino's *Morgante* (both sides), and the most humiliating for Macho, Maria Barbola, the dwarf in *Las Meninas*.

The Sisters were also quick to hit Pedro. He would get into fights with other boys who bullied him. A day did not pass without Pedro having to defend himself from pushing or shoving or having his food taken from him. Three boys—Morgan Thatch, Roberto Henrick, and Justo Cofresi—took turns roughing him up. Besides taking some of Pedro's food, they made him run errands for them, and took any money he made on chores.

When he no longer could stand their torture and abuse, he decided he had to do something. In a furious fit of rebellious anger, he beat Thatch, the biggest of the trio, with a broom handle and bit him on the thigh. After that day, Thatch and the other two backed off, but this outburst of violence horrified the nuns. Mother Superior called him Macho as a derisive taunt, and soon it became his nickname. From then on, they felt compelled to check his anger and violence by beating him at any sign of rebellion or protest. They hit him with rulers and switches, slapped him without warning, pulled him by the ears and hair, and sent his bruised body to bed without supper.

The nuns' treatment was unbearable, but it made him stronger. Their beatings only made him more resolved to escape. He led their contempt slide off him like rain off a leaf. He followed his daily routine, the years blending with the seamless summer that is life on a tropical island. He waited for an opportunity. He waited until his voice deepened and his body reached its maximum, limited size. He waited until a farmer on the way to the capital stopped to rest by the road passing the convent.

The jibaro parked his ox cart by a ceiba tree, where he leaned to eat lunch. Macho was in the garden, up a tree picking avocados, and he knew this was his one chance. He climbed down and ran with the canvas bag of avocados toward the ox cart. While the farmer relieved himself against the tree, Macho ran behind the ox cart and jumped in, wedging his body between two thick bundles of sugar cane. Soon, he was rolling on the ox cart toward the capital, smiling and crying. The swaying of the cart and the jibaro's sad songs sent him into a deep sleep.

The trip took days and he slept most of the way. He was sleeping when the jibaro woke him up, screaming at him to get off his cart, beating him with a cane stalk. Macho blocked the blows with his little legs, rolled off the cart, and ran down the road, hugging the bag of avocados. The jibaro had dropped him in the center of Rio Piedras by the market. The dusty streets were full of merchants and buyers; stalls loaded with sugar cane, rum, tobacco, hides, meats and sausages, fruits, roots, and vegetables. On the trip he had eaten a few of the avocados and sugar cane. He became aware of how hungry he was and decided to sell the remaining avocados to get some money.

The sight of a dwarf juggling avocados as he hawked them drew attention and, within minutes, he had sold the entire bag. He sold the last one to a man with a large brim hat, a headband covering his shaven head underneath. By his clothes, Macho knew he had money but the dirt on his disheveled clothing, the beaten hat, the unpolished boots, told him this man lived hard and didn't care much about appearances. The man was amused by Macho's tenacity; how he bargained for the best price. How he used his stature to advantage, making people laugh, bringing them in, making them feel good to buy another avocado when they probably only wanted one.

You're a good salesman, he told him.

I'm hungry, responded Macho, shrugging, slipping the coins into his pocket. At this, the man smiled, nodding.

How about you work for me, he said. That way you won't be hungry.

Doing what?

Making people happy.

Macho looked at him suspiciously, but he was alone in a city he didn't know, and he felt it couldn't be worse than the convent.

His boss, Miguel Henriquez, had various businesses, all focusing on what he claimed was "getting people things that are hard to get." He started Macho on the ginger run, distributing the spice to local brothels, including some he owned. Ginger was in demand as an aphrodisiac by the hookers and johns. Sometimes he brought in the weekly supply of rum using the city's underground tunnels, which his size allowed to navigate quickly. It was easy work as long as he did not get caught with the merchandise.

As a bonus, he received free access to the women, who grew to like him because he was always happy, and they knew he would never hurt them. One brothel, La Casa Blanca, became his home. After a hard day, he welcomed its shadowy warmth and velvety decor. The laughter and smiles. The shots of rum burning his throat. At the convent, he fell asleep to stark, damp silence. Here, it was rhythmic creaking of old mattresses, moaning, and the nearby waves that put him to sleep.

Macho became Henriquez's companion on his travels. His boss sailed around the Caribbean, and he wanted the dwarf by his side on every transaction. During a tobacco deal, Henriquez's counterpart, a lanky Frenchman with a crooked scar running down his nose and between his eyes, kept looking at Macho even as he spoke. When the negotiation turned heated, the Frenchman slammed the table.

This damn dwarf displeases me. Tell him to leave, he yelled.

Henriquez sat back and smiled. He's my traveling companion and most trusted confidant. You insult me with your request.

The Frenchmen narrowed his gaze at Macho, gulped a shot of rum and slapped the cup against the table. Fine, fine. Let's settle this business and be done with it.

Henriquez quoted a higher price for the tobacco and the Frenchmen agreed. Later that night, celebrating at La Casa Blanca, Henriquez tossed Macho a gold coin. Go ahead, Machito, he said. Go celebrate your God-given gift. And he toasted to Macho the Dwarf and laughed. All the others laughed and sang "Mi Vino Tan Querido." Macho went to bed.

In Cartagena, a Spanish trader wanted to include Macho in the deal. He persisted, raising the price, but Henriquez refused. A few days later, while delivering ginger and rum, two men grabbed Macho and threw him in a burlap sack. He found himself in the trader's home.

Your master seems very fond of you, little man. Let's see how much, the Spaniard said, smiling and showing rotten teeth.

The ransom was a considerable amount. After paying it, Henriquez assigned a bodyguard to accompany the dwarf everywhere he went.

You're very valuable to me, Machito. I paid a lot for your freedom, so now it belongs to me.

Macho's life continued as before. When he wasn't traveling with Don Miguel, he supplied ginger and rum to the brothels and delivered special goods such as cigars or brandy to preferred clients, who felt privileged to have Henriquez's lucky dwarf service them.

He kept the room at La Casa Blanca and enjoyed the company of the ladies there. But now he had Barajas, the bodyguard, accompanying him everywhere. He could not even relieve himself without the tall, fat criollo watching him.

Barajas had studied in Spain, felt himself superior to the illiterate islanders. To him, having to guard a dwarf was disgraceful and he intended to make the most of the insulting situation. On the first outing, he punched Macho in the face and took money from what he had collected. If you don't want a beating next time, he said, you know what you have to do. So, every time out, Macho had to find a way to make up the deficit with his commissions or savings. After a long period together, Barajas grew to like Macho, and even felt pity for him.

You're a criollo like me, he told him. We should work together. Henriquez has so much money he won't miss a few gold coins. He looked around and leaned into Macho. Friends tell me his operations are falling apart. Macho nodded as if he had a choice. From that moment on, the criollo and the dwarf spent the stolen money getting drunk, gambling and dancing with prostitutes.

This working relationship did not escape Henriquez's network of informants. On their next trip, Henriquez stabbed Barajas in his meaty buttocks and had him thrown overboard in shark-filled waters. After the men watched the sharks fighting over the last piece of Barajas's corpulent leg, Henriquez turned to Macho.

You ungrateful little bastard, he said. If it wasn't for me, you'd be begging in the streets. Macho stood before him in tears. You can't even make a decent meal for sharks. I have other plans for you. He snapped his fingers and the first mate took Macho down to the brig and there he stayed until they reached port.

Early in the morning, they dragged him from the cell and injected him with something. Before he fell asleep, Macho looked up at the bright daylight and heard Henriquez's laughter. When he awoke, he was strapped to a beach chair, one among many lined in rows inside an old, retrofitted Army transport plane. The men occupying the chairs were snoring, others talking in Spanish.

His stomach rumbled; his tongue and lips smacked for water. Through blurry eyes, he saw a large balding man with a pencil mustache. He walked toward the back of the plane. His frown was the last thing Macho saw before slipping back to sleep.

Someone nudged him to get up. He dragged himself out of the chair and marched down the aircraft stairs with the others. Macho looked around and saw that other men had brought suitcases or personal bundles and he had nothing. They gathered the men in trucks that took them to a combine with several white blocky buildings. The balding man spoke to them with a bull horn. Call me Moscoso, he said. There was snickering because his name sounded like mocoso, meaning snotty, or a bratty child. He glared at them with narrowed eyes. His thin lips kept smirking, sneering, making his thin mustache wiggle like a worm.

I'm your crew chief, he said, his voice rising. From now on, your life is in my hands. You do not get paid without me. You do not eat without me. You do not shit or piss without my permission. You cannot get laid without me. If you're sick, I will find you a doctor. You will be charged for food, lodging, and incidentals. Any problems you come directly to me. Understand? Everyone nodded. If you give me any problems, I will send you back to your wretched lives and make sure you never work around here again.

They started work that same day, picking mushrooms from hundreds of stacked tiers. These tiers contained soil beds that ran yards across the massive plant. Macho's height allowed him to access the mushrooms between the cramped tiers easier. At the higher tiers, the task became harder since it required balancing on the narrow two-plank catwalk high above the ground. Falling or stumbling was a possibility because inside the building it was always dark and humid.

That's what happened to Porfirio, an undocumented worker from Mexico. He slipped and sustained an open fracture on his leg, and Moscoso wouldn't take him to the hospital because he hadn't earned enough to pay a trip to the doctor. When the leg worsened, the crew chief finally drove him to see a doctor, making Porfirio sign a promissory note for the bills. At the hospital they had to amputate the leg. The company sent him back to Mexico.

After a fifteen-hour shift, Macho and the others retired to the barracks, where they slept on iron bunk beds jammed into a small dark room. Since their salaries were not enough to pay for local housing, the company provided workers with lodging and deducted the rent from their pay, along with food, mattresses and sheets, cigarettes and bottles of overpriced liquor, and the occasional escort. Macho's room had broken windows and heaters with frayed wiring. They shared one bathroom that had a toilet with no seat and a blackened bowl that often clogged and overflowed for weeks before getting cleaned. The stinging odor of urine assaulted their noses daily.

During any season, several men would become sick. They coughed, spit up globs of bloody mucus, became emaciated or developed nagging back pain. Impetigo was always a risk; nosebleeds, normal. They had allergic reactions to pesticides and chemicals they inhaled because they didn't have masks. No one complained because a trip to the clinic or hospital would cost hours of pay or worse, a trip back home.

On the first payday, Moscoso pulled Macho out of the line and informed him he was not receiving a check. After paying for your room and other incidentals, the remainder of what you earned goes to Henriquez.

Macho stared at Moscoso, shocked. That's not fair, he said.

Not my problem, the crew chief said. That was the deal.

How long before I pay him back?

Moscoso laughed. Freedom is an expensive commodity, little man.

I refuse to work, then, he said.

You don't work, I send you back to Henriquez. And you know if you're no use to him, he'll find a way to end your contract to his liking. He dismissed him with a snap of his head and a sharp "go."

That night when the others celebrated, Macho lay on his sinking, moldy mattress. He cursed the day he met Henriquez. He wondered what his life would have been like if he had stayed at the convent. Perhaps he could have taken over Cristobal's job. That seemed so long ago, and the island so far way, that returning to the Sisters was a futile thought. He had to find a way to escape. But how could he without money?

As he thought about his sad situation, Marín, another Puerto Rican worker, brought him a paper cup filled with whiskey. The others all knew about his getting stiffed by Moscoso and felt bad. They raised a few bucks for him, and he was happy. Drink up, 'mano. Don't let those cabrones get to you. Macho toasted to his words and took a sip. Marín took a wrapper out of his shirt pocket and unraveled some mushrooms. He had found them on one of his walks into the countryside. That was how Marín escaped, by taking long walks around the surrounding forest areas, reciting poetry to the wind. Macho made a face. The last thing he wanted to see were mushrooms.

Marín laughed. These are not like the ones we kill ourselves picking, oh no. These are magic mushrooms.

Here, he said, offering a piece of the straw-colored shroom. Eat it. Like this, raw?

Yes, Marín laughed. It will make you see marvelous things.

Curious, and a bit tipsy from the whiskey, he popped the piece into his mouth.

Soon, he was walking in a forest, lush with vegetation. Marín walked with him but wandered off reciting poetry to the trees and they separated. Macho came across an enormous mushroom. He suddenly craved more mushrooms and decided to climb the stem to reach the cap. At the top, he saw a massive, white mansion. It seemed like an inviting house, so he decided to see who lived there. As he walked toward the mansion, he noticed that he wasn't a dwarf any longer. He stopped to touch his arms and legs, his head, to marvel in the transformation. He was taller and could walk normally. On a whim, he darted and ran fast toward the mansion, crying from the joy. Closer to the mansion, he saw cannons protruding from every window. The door was open, and he let himself in.

What a beautiful house, he thought, as he ran his fingers through the fine woodwork and peeked at the paintings of white, somber men staring at him. It was a house full of expensive collectibles, each one, on closer inspection, containing the faint smell of blood and grounded bones. He startled to see a giant sleeping across a huge bed, his snoring rattling the windows. A slender, somewhat wiry man, he had thick white hair and a little wispy gray beard. His frown and curling lip gave Macho the impression that he was in the middle of a bad dream.

Scanning the room, three shiny, gold objects caught his attention: a small chest overrunning with gold coins; a statuette of a calf; and an electric guitar. He had never seen anything like these objects before and their glitter hypnotized him. The giant stirred from his slumber and shot up from the bed. Sniffing, he yelled, Mongrel blood. Macho clutched the chest full of coins and ran out the door, running until he reached the mushroom and climbed down.

He laughed and rejoiced in his newly found treasure. When he grabbed the coins, they were soft and pliable. He bit into one and his teeth went through the gold tin foil to the chocolate underneath. Hungry, he tore the rest of the tinfoil wrapping and gorged on the chocolate. He fell asleep, content with his new, long body and full stomach, but later he woke and needed to eat again, so he decided to steal the golden calf. Up he went again, and the giant was now watching a football game on television. He was so absorbed by the game he didn't notice Macho behind him, walking to the bedroom. Macho grabbed the golden calf and tip-toed back to the door and outside.

No sooner had he descended and placed the golden calf on the ground, a cloud surrounded it. When the smoke subsided, the statuette had transformed into a real calf and just as quickly it took a dump right in front of Macho's feet. The calf's droppings glittered and, as Macho looked closer, he realized they were gold nuggets. Amazed, he picked them up. Easily, twenty-four carats, he thought. He sat to contemplate how rich he would become. The many things he could buy. A certain blissful feeling took over his body.

But his stomach growled and that feeling turned into despair at not knowing when his next meal would come. The gold was useless in this forest, he thought. His hunger intensified and with a large rock he killed the calf. He skinned the calf, marinated it with an adobo made from the surrounding herbs and spices, built a fire, and roasted the meat on a handmade rotating pit. Sated from the tender and tasty meat, he fell asleep only to wake up feeling a profound boredom mixed with sadness. He decided music would get him out of his funk. He climbed the mushroom again, this time to steal the guitar.

The giant was drinking bourbon and counting gold coins. He stacked them up in tall columns, then as he cackled with glee, slapped them down. Macho had never seen so much money in one place before. Every inch of the floor covered with coins and piled stacks of Benjamins and Grovers. Macho moved closer, and the giant was rolling naked on the money, snorting with laughter, humping the stacks of bills. The golden Gibson Les Paul leaned against the wall closest to the door, a few feet from Macho's reach.

In a dash, he seized it. The giant jumped up, sniffing. Mongrel blood, he yelled. Macho took off through the door and toward the mushroom, the giant in pursuit. With those long legs he'll catch me in no time, he thought, now fearful for his life. You son of a bitch, the giant yelled. You stole my money and calf, but I'll be damn if you take my Les Paul. Macho had never run faster in his life. He slung the guitar strap across his chest and descended.

At the bottom, he saw two woodsmen carrying their axes. He yelled to them to lend him an axe to cut the mushroom stem. He blurted his predicament and the two men started arguing whether it was wise to do it. One of them, Barbosa, kept saying Macho was at fault for stealing from the giant who had done him no wrong.

You should ask forgiveness from the giant and seek friendship and together you can help each other.

Concepción looked at his companion as if he were mad. Are you serious? That giant has terrorized everyone down here for centuries.

He didn't steal anything from the giant that didn't belong to us in the first place. Here take my axe and let's rid ourselves of that bastard once and for all.

They continued arguing and at that moment the giant, drunk as he was, lost his grip and fell to the ground, landing on all three of them.

When Macho's head cleared, it was early morning. He could not sleep thinking about the vision he had witnessed. It kept replaying in his mind. Outside, fat raindrops plopped against the concrete walkways and splattered the cracked windows held together with duct tape. The wind rushed in as they prepared for another day of work. The coughing and other bodily sounds began. Macho covered his head with the worn blanket and tried to erase the vision from his head. But he kept seeing the giant falling on him, squashing him, and remembered the sensation of suffocation as he gasped for air. It seemed too real.

During work, flashbacks from his trip slowed his work. Moscoso kept telling him he was falling behind quota. He didn't care about work anymore. He didn't care about anything. What difference did it make, anyway? He was not getting paid, and so what if Moscoso send him back to the island? Maybe it was for the best if they fed him to the sharks.

Being in this frame of mind for months, Macho drifted into the union meetings. There had been talk about organizing the mushroom workers into a union despite strict threats from Moscoso and the owners not to attempt it. He thought being around other people would break him out of the doldrums. But at the meetings, the fiery organizer, Campos, electrified them with his words, and Macho, like the others, began to believe their condition could improve. Campos said things all of them knew and felt but could not express as well.

The workers decided to strike. They pooled money to buy food and supplies to last a few months. Then on a bright March day, they locked themselves in their barracks and refused to work. Campos gave Moscoso their demands to take to the owners.

This is what the owners think of your demands, he said as he ripped up the paper. Be back at work tomorrow morning or we'll drag you out. You lost a day's wages, cabrones.

We've received their answer, compañeros, Campos told them with weariness and concern in his dark, piercing eyes. They will force us out. They will not reason with us. Be assured that they will send those who are undocumented back. That's what they do. I don't know about you, but I'm not going to work in this stinking hole anymore. And neither is anyone else.

With that, he took a can of gasoline and starting splashing everything in the rooms. Get out, run, Campos yelled before he threw the lighted match. The workers rushed out the door. Along with others, Macho went into the harvesting area and started tearing down the tiers, throwing the mushrooms to the ground, smashing them with their boots. Soon smoke spiraled from there, and they ran out coughing into the summer sun. Running to the main gate, they saw Moscoso cradling a shotgun in front of dozens of armed men. The workers circled, looking for another escape route, but there was no time. Bullets and buckshot flew. They ran for cover or toward the fences to climb and make a run for it. Macho ran and slid under the stilts of the raised supplies warehouse.

From there, he saw Moscoso's men beat and shoot down his fellow workers. He saw them drag bodies and throw them into wagons that drove away at night. His men handcuffed others who the local police turned over to the INS. In pitch blackness, he crawled from under his hideout. The air was thick with fumes of burned gasoline, wood, and mushrooms mixed with the metallic smell of blood. He ran past blackened barracks and piled debris toward the back of the combine, where he climbed a fence and jumped to freedom.

He found the highway to Big City. Drivers will usually stop for a dwarf looking for a ride, Macho soon realized. On the way, Macho met up with Ela's Circus, a small traveling troupe owned by a Polish woman from Poznań, and they gave him a job. His past training as a juggler and jester came in handy, but mostly he cleaned up after the elephants and other animals. When the circus folded, Macho decided to stay in Big City, where they played their last venue.

He took up a job busing and cleaning at the Shining Star, a bar owned by a pockmarked, heavy set Puerto Rican named Romero. Romero felt sorry for his countryman and let him work doing menial tasks. Macho received minimum wage, tips, free meals, and drinks. Way better than either Henriquez or the mushroom farm. Then, Romero read an article on dwarf tossing and convinced Macho to participate to bring in business. You'll make more tips, he said, in the excited, staccato way he talked. Macho agreed. What else could he do? He had reached the point when life offered limited choices and the future promised only brutal work and decisions made by others.

He became the most popular dwarf on the circuit. People came down to the Shining Star to enjoy themselves watching Macho in his jogging suit and helmet being tossed across padded mats. He was proud co-owner of the record at the bar, eleven feet nine inches. On nights not being tossed, he worked at the bowling competitions. The bowling was a bit harder. Being thrown on a skateboard down a bowling alley to hit wooden pins was not as much fun as flying across the room. What made Macho so popular was his lightness and his amiability while being tossed around. Nothing seemed to bother him. He just went along with it, whatever it was. And he was a born entertainer, always down to have a good time. He became the poster boy of dwarf tossing and bowling. He even granted interviews defending his status as a "missile" for these "sports."

Whenever another petition to place a referendum outlawing these activities circulated, the bar owners asked him to speak against them. And he did. What business was it to others if dwarfs wanted to be tossed and bowled? He made a decent living from entertaining folks. It's all about having a good time, Macho would tell reporters. More seriously he would say, There aren't exactly many jobs for us little people out here, you know what I mean? We're small and we need to deal with that reality.

With his popularity came an increase in award money, donations, and tips, and Macho was finally able to rent his own apartment in El Barrio. Life was as best can be for a little person in a world of giants. But as the Hector Lavoe song goes, "Todo tiene su final." With more money came more spending. Macho believed in working to live, and he lived hard and reckless. When the popularity of those activities that fueled his livelihood fizzled, he found himself again in debt.

He owed so much that he couldn't pay rent and was evicted. He roamed the streets of El Barrio begging for food and drinks. The tragedy that had been his life was not enough compensation for those who held his IOUs. One day while rummaging through a McDonald's dumpster, some men picked him up and tossed him into a van. He was drugged and hours later found himself in a desert, buried up to his neck. Macho searched the flat terrain for his captors to return, to tell him this was a joke, a final warning to pay up. Above, vultures circled, casting shadows with thunderous wings, while screeching and waiting.

ACKNOWLEDGMENTS

Every book is a collaborative effort, so I would like to thank everyone who played a role in assisting me in this collection. Lisa Sánchez González, your research into the Puerto Rican children sent to the Carlisle Indian Industrial School not only inspired me to write one of the stories, but it also served as the creative impetus for the entire collection. Thanks to SUNY Plattsburgh for granting me a sabbatical so I could get across the finish line. My wonderful Plattsburgh writing group, thanks for the feedback, especially colleagues and friends, Aimee Baker and Elizabeth Cohen, whose excellent readings and critiques helped me revise many of these stories.

Tom Lutz, what a great editor you are. Your insightful recommendations have undoubtedly made this book better. Thanks to everyone at LARB and UC Riverside, especially Alex Espinoza, for creating the Tomás Rivera Book Prize. Luis Alberto Urrea, a million thanks for judging *Migrations* worthy of being its first recipient. I am truly humbled and honored to receive an award named after someone whom I deeply respect as a writer and educator. Special thanks to Sonia Ali and Nanda Dyssou for all of your hard work. Leila Aguilera, your cover is a fabulous, artful representation of the blurry vision in my head. Thank you so much for adding that needed touch to the collection.

As always, thanks to my family—Lee, my life partner, and my two sons, Alex and Julian—for your support and love. Jules, working with you on "Rip & Reck" was my biggest pleasure in writing this book. Thanks so much for your editorial feedback and your hip-hop expertise. To my extended family, I'm so blessed to have you all in my life.